Christmas Classics

Christmas Classics

The Story Behind 40 Favorite Carols

David McLaughlan

BARBOUR
PUBLISHING

ISBN 978-1-60260-836-8

Published by Barbour Publishing, Inc., P.O. Box 719,
Uhrichsville, Ohio 44683 www.barbourbooks.com

*Our mission is to publish and distribute inspirational
products offering exceptional value and biblical
encouragement to the masses.*

Member of the
Evangelical Christian
Publishers Association

Printed in the United States of America.

Introduction

How does a carol become a "Christmas classic"?

The best way is to touch the hearts of people living different kinds of lives in different parts of the world, over many, many generations. No simple task! But if the carol is about hope, love, and redemption—and it's matched with a beautiful melody—it *will* stir something in the human heart, whether the listener is a fourteenth-century European or a twenty-first-century American.

Many of the carols in this collection were first sung before the invention of the printing press. If they were written down at all, it would have been with quill and ink and available to only an educated few. The printing press brought these carols to a much wider audience.

Then came recordings, on cylinders, 78s, LPs, tapes, and CDs. Carols could now be heard as well as read, all around the world.

Now we live in the Internet age—and carols still feature strongly in the new media.

Internet searches reveal sometimes *millions* of pages dedicated to songs of the Nativity. These Internet "hits" enabled us to compile a ranking of the top forty carols for Christmas.

Everyone has personal favorites, and no two lists will ever agree. But for now, sit back and enjoy the who, what, when, where, and why of our forty top selections. Celebrate with us the fact that modern technology has enabled more people than ever to find and sing classic songs of worship and joy at Christmastime.

Thou Didst Leave Thy Throne

Thou didst leave Thy throne and Thy kingly crown,
When Thou camest to earth for me;
But in Bethlehem's home was there found no room
For Thy holy nativity.

O come to my heart, Lord Jesus,
There is room in my heart for Thee.

Heaven's arches rang when the angels sang,
Proclaiming Thy royal degree;
But of lowly birth didst Thou come to earth,
And in great humility.

O come to my heart, Lord Jesus,
There is room in my heart for Thee.

The foxes found rest, and the birds their nest
In the shade of the forest tree;
But Thy couch was the sod, O Thou Son of God,
In the deserts of Galilee.

O come to my heart, Lord Jesus,
There is room in my heart for Thee.

Thou camest, O Lord, with the living Word,
That should set Thy people free;
But with mocking scorn and with crown of thorn,
They bore Thee to Calvary.

O come to my heart, Lord Jesus,
There is room in my heart for Thee.

When the heav'ns shall ring, and her choirs shall
    sing,
At Thy coming to victory,
Let Thy voice call me home, saying "Yet there is room,
There is room at My side for thee."

My heart shall rejoice, Lord Jesus,
When Thou comest and callest for me.

Who?

Emily Elizabeth Steele Elliott was twenty-eight when she wrote "Thou Didst Leave Thy Throne." She was the daughter of the Anglican rector (later bishop) Edward Elliott.

The music was composed specifically for Elliott's words by leading English organist Timothy Richard Matthews.

What?

"Thou Didst Leave Thy Throne" is a song of appreciation, apology, and love. Its author stands amazed at how much the Lord gave up for us; she is horrified by how mankind treated Him; and she offers her heart and her whole self in recompense.

Though Emily Elliott was a published writer and earned an income from her work, "Thou Didst Leave Thy Throne" was emphatically not written for profit. Published privately, it was meant to be sung by the children of her father's church as a way to teach those young casualties of the Industrial Revolution that someone loved them and there were better days to come.

When?

Written in 1864, the year before the American Civil War ended. The music was composed in 1876, the same year Queen Victoria was declared Empress of India in Great Britain.

Where?

Emily Elliott spent the first part of her life (and did much of her writing, including this hymn) in Brighton, England, where her father was rector of St. Mark's church.

Situated on the south coast of England,

Brighton was a fishing village until a rail link made it a fashionable holiday destination for the wealthier set of English society.

Though the town became more "gentrified," increased industrialization meant that Brighton was never short of poor, uneducated, and needy people.

Why?

Emily Elliott came from a family of hymn writers. Her father, uncle, and two aunts wrote sacred songs. Her aunt Charlotte composed the famous hymn "Just As I Am." So, it was probably to be expected that young Emily would express her faith and feelings through hymn writing.

In Victorian society, it was not uncommon for ladies of a certain status to spend time and money aiding the poor. In a way, it demonstrated their status, piety, and wealth.

As the daughter of a rector, Emily Elliott was unlikely to have been wealthy, and her devotion to the poor seems to have come from a higher place. She worked for many years with "fallen women" in rescue missions and had a passion for the relatively new Sunday school movement, in which children were taught reading and writing as well as religion.

39 INFANT HOLY, INFANT LOWLY

Infant holy, Infant lowly,
For His bed a cattle stall;
Oxen lowing, little knowing,
Christ the Babe is Lord of all.

Swift are winging angels singing,
Noels ringing, tidings bringing:
Christ the Babe is Lord of all.
Flocks were sleeping, shepherds keeping
Vigil till the morning new
Saw the glory, heard the story,
Tidings of a Gospel true.

Thus rejoicing, free from sorrow,
Praises voicing, greet the morrow:
Christ the Babe was born for you.

Who?

Piotr Poweski was a Polish orphan. He became a tutor, then a rector, before joining the Society of Jesus. His missionary zeal in countering the Protestant Reformation inspired the nickname Skarga, or "Accuser."

Edith Margaret Gellibrand Reed turned Poweski's hymn "W Zlobie Lezy" into the English "Infant Holy, Infant Lowly." Reed was a traveler and an editor of music magazines. When she died at forty-eight, she was described as "a teacher and friend of children."

What?

"Infant Holy, Infant Lowly" washes over the listener like the waves of the sea, gradually building to crescendos in the middle and at the end. But these crescendos, when they come, are surprisingly gentle, summing up, we might suppose, Poweski's and Reed's opinions of Christ—all-powerful, yet all-loving.

The words lead the listener to two vitally important aspects of Christ's time on earth—that though He was born, lived, and died in the humblest of circumstances, He was still the Lord of all; and that He did all that He did willingly for the ones who will hear His message and willingly accept His love.

When?

Probably written in the latter half of the sixteenth century, when the Protestant Reformation was challenging papal authority. Mary Tudor briefly restored Catholicism in England before her successor, Elizabeth I, made it a Protestant country.

Translated into English in 1921, as Europe and America recovered from World War I.

Where?

Piotr Poweski was born in Grojec, Poland, studied in Italy, preached in Lithuania, and became a favorite of the Polish court. The carol could have been written in any of those places, but the choice of language and its popularity with the Polish people make Poland the most obvious choice.

Edith Reed was born in Middlesex, England.

Why?

For Poweski, "W Zlobie Lezy," or "Lying in a Manger," was a retelling of the Nativity that was simple enough to be used in his preaching, yet powerful enough to be remembered by those who sang it.

Edith Reed was a musician and music teacher. She was a writer of "mystery" plays, which concentrated on the miracle of God becoming human—the same theme as Poweski's hymn.

After World War I, England became a new home for many Polish soldiers who had fought with the British army. They brought their customs

and songs with them. Through them, Reed was able
to hear the original words and melody as Poweski
had written them.

38 THERE'S A SONG IN THE AIR

There's a song in the air!
There's a star in the sky!
There's a mother's deep prayer
And a baby's low cry!
And the star rains its fire
While the beautiful sing,
For the manger of Bethlehem
Cradles a King!
There's a tumult of joy
O'er the wonderful birth,
For the virgin's sweet boy
Is the Lord of the earth.
Ay! the star rains its fire
While the beautiful sing,
For the manger of Bethlehem
Cradles a King!

In the light of that star
Lie the ages impearled;

And that song from afar
Has swept over the world.
Every hearth is aflame,
And the beautiful sing
In the homes of the nations
That Jesus is King!

We rejoice in the light,
And we echo the song
That comes down through the night
From the heavenly throng.
Ay! we shout to the lovely
Evangel they bring,
And we greet in his cradle
Our Saviour and King!

Who?

Josiah Gilbert Holland was born in 1819 to a family suffering hard times. Working in a factory as a child, to help make ends meet, may have caused the health problems that led Holland to drop out of high school. Nevertheless, he later qualified as a doctor (though his practice failed) and went on to become a successful novelist, journalist, poet, and magazine editor.

Two years after Holland died, Karl P. Harrington, a teacher and university professor, put the words of "There's a Song in the Air" to music.

What?

The first two verses of this hymn focus on the wonder of the night when the star shone down on a humble manger that held the eternal King and celebrate the event of His birth.

The last two verses, added later, show Christ as the culmination of all that has gone before and describe how His "song" will spread throughout the world until each of us sings it back to "our Saviour and King."

When?

First published in 1872, the year of the Great Boston Fire and the same year that Susan B. Anthony voted for the first time (despite it being illegal for women to do so).

Where?

Josiah Holland was Massachusetts born and bred. His affection for the state inspired him to write a history of western Massachusetts. He achieved a fair amount of success as a journalist there, enough to fund a trip to Europe; but he spent the latter part of his life in New York City, where he edited *Scribner's Monthly* and wrote three novels and several volumes of poems. One of those volumes, *The Marble Prophecy*, contains the poem "There's a Song in the Air" (originally titled "A Christmas Carol").

Why?

Josiah Holland's faith shines through in his writings. He dedicated a book of "advice to the young" to minister and social reformer Henry Ward Beecher. He referred often to God, "the great Master," and His instructions for us. His beliefs may have been of the everyday kind, informing his decisions and his work, but of course there is no such thing as an ordinary faith. Through his love of the Lord, Josiah Holland left us an extraordinary gift in this beautiful carol.

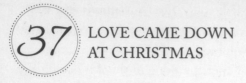

37 LOVE CAME DOWN AT CHRISTMAS

Love came down at Christmas,
Love all lovely, love divine;
Love was born at Christmas,
Star and angels gave the sign.
Worship we the Godhead,
Love incarnate, love divine;
Worship we our Jesus:
But wherewith for sacred sign?
Love shall be our token,
Love shall be yours and love be mine,
Love to God and to all men,
Love for plea and gift and sign.

Who?

Christina Georgina Rossetti was the daughter of Gabriel Rossetti, a political dissenter who fled Naples for refuge in London. Her brothers Dante and William helped to establish the Pre-Raphaelite Brotherhood, a new artistic movement that relied heavily on classical and religious themes. Christina was the model for two of Dante Rossetti's paintings of the young Mary, mother of Jesus.

In an age when a young woman's best option

was a suitable marriage, Christina stayed in the family home, making a name (and an income) for herself through her poetry.

The hymn "In the Bleak Midwinter" was also originally a Christina Rossetti poem.

What?

Originally called "Christmastide," the poem that came to be the hymn "Love Came Down at Christmas" slips delicately and directly to the heart of Christ's mission on earth: that mankind should love God and each other.

Acknowledging that God had become human for us, Rossetti in her poem asks how we might repay that gift.

A token was needed, she thought, a sign to God that we were His. And what better token could we offer than obedience to His great commandment to love. Our "sacred sign," she decided, could only be love "to God and all men."

When?

First published in 1885, the same year that Mark Twain's *Adventures of Huckleberry Finn* first appeared in print; and the Statue of Liberty, a gift from France, arrived in New York harbor. That same year, Karl Benz patented the world's first custom-built automobile.

Where?

Although her family moved to Britain from Italy, Christina Rossetti was born and died in London, living under the reign of Queen Victoria from the age of seven.

Time Flies: A Reading Diary, which includes the text of "Love Came Down at Christmas," was published by the Society for Promoting Christian Knowledge and begins with a quote from James Montgomery that each day passed was "a day's march nearer home."

Why?

In her midteens, Rossetti suffered a nervous breakdown brought on largely by her family's desperate circumstances. Faith became a solace that would stay with her and play a major part in her life, influencing not only her poetry but also her voluntary work. Rossetti spent more than a decade working with no pay at a London mission for "fallen" women.

This kind of "unseemly" behavior in a society obsessed by appearances may have damaged Rossetti's marriage prospects—but her love for the Lord carried her through.

36 HERE WE COME A-WASSAILING

Here we come a-wassailing
Among the leaves so green;
Here we come a-wand'ring
So fair to be seen.

Chorus
Love and joy come to you,
And to you your wassail too;
And God bless you and send you a Happy New Year
And God send you a Happy New Year.

Our wassail cup is made
Of the rosemary tree,
And so is your beer
Of the best barley.

Chorus

We are not daily beggars
That beg from door to door;
But we are neighbours' children,
Whom you have seen before.

Chorus

Call up the butler of this house,
Put on his golden ring.
Let him bring us up a glass of beer,
And better we shall sing.

Chorus

We have got a little purse
Of stretching leather skin;
We want a little of your money
To line it well within.

Chorus

Bring us out a table
And spread it with a cloth;
Bring us out a mouldy cheese,
And some of your Christmas loaf.

Chorus

God bless the master of this house
Likewise the mistress too,
And all the little children
That round the table go.

Chorus

Good master and good mistress,
While you're sitting by the fire,
Pray think of us poor children
Who are wandering in the mire.

Who?

There are too many versions of "Here We Come A-Wassailing" to be able to pinpoint any one writer.

The term *wassail*, or "wass-heil," is a Saxon greeting that came to England with fifth-century Saxon mercenaries and settlers.

What?

As Christmas carols go, "Here We Come A-Wassailing" has to be one of the more secular. Most versions don't even mention Christmas, focusing instead on a happy new year.

Given that is was traditionally sung to wealthy homeowners by agricultural workers and children from poor families, the carol could be seen as a call to Christian charity, inviting those with plenty to share food, drink, money, and even warmth in the midst of a cold winter with those who had little of any of those things. More likely, its popularity lies in the cheery tune and the excuse to have a good time, inviting everyone else (especially those with plenty of warm and spicy alcoholic drink) to join in!

When?

Thought to be a traditional seventeenth-century English carol, it first appeared in print in 1871, the year that three major British universities first allowed student admissions without a religious examination, and Henry Morton Stanley found "lost" missionary David Livingstone in Africa.

Where?

"Here We Come A-Wassailing" is sung all over the English-speaking world today, but traditionally, it is firmly associated with the southwestern counties of England.

Why?

In times gone by, apple growers and their wives, usually fueled by copious amounts of cider, would invade their orchards on Christmas Eve (Twelfth Night in some places), making as much noise as they could to scare away evil spirits.

Sometimes they would share their libation with the trees and wish them good health (which is what "wassail" means). Alternatively, the husband would rant at the trees, telling them they were worthless. Then he would shake his ax at them, insisting he was going to chop them down for firewood. His wife would follow on, assuring each tree it would be safe—if only it could give a good crop of apples in the next year!

The tradition moved from the countryside into

the towns (without the axes), and people would sing from door to door, wishing their neighbors God's blessings and a good new year. The invitation to give the carolers a drink at each door meant that such carol singing frequently got out of control. Many towns eventually banned the practice.

 ## BRING A TORCH, JEANETTE, ISABELLA

Bring a torch, Jeanette, Isabella
Bring a torch, to the cradle run!
It is Jesus, good folk of the village;
Christ is born and Mary's calling;
Ah, ah, beautiful is the Mother
Ah, ah, beautiful is her Son!

It is wrong when the Child is sleeping
It is wrong to talk so loud;
Silence, all, as you gather around.
Lest your noise should waken Jesus.
Hush, hush, see how fast He slumbers!
Hush, hush, see how fast He sleeps!

Hasten now, good folk of the village;
Hasten now the Christ Child to see.

You will find Him asleep in the manger;
Quietly come and whisper softly,
Hush, hush, peacefully now He slumbers.
Hush, hush, peacefully now He sleeps.

Softly to the little stable.
Softly for a moment come;
Look and see how charming is Jesus
How He is white, His cheeks are rosy!
Hush, hush, see how the Child is sleeping;
Hush, hush, see how He smiles in his dreams.

Who?

The authorship and date of this piece is disputed. In 1901, Julien Tiersot published *French Carols*, which included "Bring a Torch, Jeanette, Isabella." The author was listed as Emile Blémont, and Tiersot indicated the carol was a version of a carol by Nicholas Saboly, who lived in the seventeenth century. Other sources suggest that the text and music were included in a compilation of Christmas songs published privately in 1553.

What?

The carol is a fantasy, but it owes its appeal to the notion of how wonderful things *might* have been. If only, as in the song, two young maids had witnessed the birth of Christ, recognized Him for who and what He was, then run to tell the whole town about Him. If only those townsfolk had gathered round, adored Him, then spread the word. If only the whole world had loved Him from the start!

Of course, the world didn't love Him. A world that generous would have had no need for Jesus.

Perhaps those who keep Him in their hearts today can be forgiven for listening to "Bring a Torch, Jeanette, Isabella" and wishing they could have been there, to stand in the flickering shadows and see His face as He smiled in His dreams.

When?
In 1553, the same year that "Bring a Torch, Jeanette, Isabella" was written, Lady Jane Grey ruled England for just nine days before abdicating in favor of Henry VIII's daughter Mary. When the Catholic Mary took the throne, Anglican clergy across the country were arrested and Roman Catholic clergy were restored.

Where?
"Bring a Torch, Jeanette, Isabella" comes from either Anjou or Burgundy in France. Children there still dress up as shepherds and milkmaids

and sing the song on their way to church on Christmas Eve.

Three hundred years after it was written, the carol crossed the channel to England. From there it traveled to America.

Why?

French nobility, like lords and ladies the world over, liked few things better than a formal dance. The melody to this carol was originally a popular dance tune, explaining why it is more upbeat than many other carols.

Nicolas Denisot, a French nobleman, was also a lawyer and a poet with a passion for songs of faith. Under the pen name Count d'Alsinois, he paid for and published a collection of Christmas carols called *The First Advent of Jesus Christ*. This compilation is said to have included the first printed copy of "Bring a Torch, Jeanette, Isabella."

34 GOOD CHRISTIAN MEN, REJOICE

Good Christian men, rejoice
With heart and soul and voice;
Give ye heed to what we say:
News! News! Jesus Christ is born today;
Ox and ass before Him bow;
And He is in the manger now.
Christ is born today! Christ is born today!

Good Christian men, rejoice,
With heart and soul and voice;
Now ye hear of endless bliss:
Joy! Joy! Jesus Christ was born for this!
He has opened the heavenly door,
And man is blest forevermore.
Christ was born for this! Christ was born for this!

Good Christian men, rejoice,
With heart and soul and voice;
Now ye need not fear the grave:
Peace! Peace! Jesus Christ was born to save!
Calls you one and calls you all,
To gain His everlasting hall.
Christ was born to save! Christ was born to save!

Who?

Heinrich Seuse (also known as Henry Suso), a German mystic "blessed" by Pope Gregory XVI.

In the mid-nineteenth century, John Mason Neale, hymn writer, doctor of divinity, and church restorationist, freely adapted Seuse's "In Dulci Jubilo" into "Good Christian Men, Rejoice."

What?

While Seuse's song simply has the angels singing in celebration of the birth of Christ, an eighteenth-century translation of his lyrics combines the angels' joy with the listener's longing to know Christ personally. "Deeply we were stained," he writes, "but Thou for us have gained the joys of heaven."

John Mason Neale's version is sung from the point of view of the angels. They remind us that Christ is born to save, and He wants to invite us all to live with Him in His everlasting home.

Surely an idea worthy of the very sweetest celebration!

When?

Written sometime in the first half of the fourteenth century, when the world was entering a little ice age. The throne of the pope was transferred from Rome in Italy to Avignon in France.

Famine and black death ravaged Europe, and the Hundred Years' War began.

Where?
Seuse studied under Meister Eckhart in the Dominican Studium Generale at Cologne, Germany. Shortly afterward, he was appointed lector (or reader) at the Dominican convent in Constance. The hymn was probably written at some point during this period.

Why?
Despite the dire state of Europe at the time, Heinrich Seuse felt that the birth of Christ was worth celebrating. Having a joyful faith and being fond of a song, he soon became known as a "troubadour of divine wisdom." He was also a practitioner of physical mortification—and reportedly not a fan of bathing.

His personality and faith seem to have overcome his circumstances, and Seuse was often described as a lovely and charismatic figure.

Not one for preaching to great crowds, he fulfilled the role of spiritual director for many individuals across western Europe.

During his spells of mortification, Seuse often had angelic visitations. It was during one of these episodes that he stumbled upon a gathering of singing angels. Well accustomed to such experiences, Seuse didn't run away like many might have. He joined in the singing and even did a little dancing. Once the angels departed, Seuse wrote down the words they had been singing and called it "In Dulci Jubilo," or "In Sweetest Rejoicing."

 ## ANGELS FROM THE REALMS OF GLORY

Angels from the realms of glory,
Wing your flight o'er all the earth;
Ye who sang creation's story
Now proclaim Messiah's birth.
Come and worship, come and worship,
Worship Christ, the newborn King.

Shepherds, in the field abiding,
Watching o'er your flocks by night,
God with us is now residing;
Yonder shines the infant light:
Come and worship, come and worship,
Worship Christ, the newborn King.

Sages, leave your contemplations,
Brighter visions beam afar;
Seek the great Desire of nations;
Ye have seen His natal star.
Come and worship, come and worship,
Worship Christ, the newborn King.

Saints, before the altar bending,
Watching long in hope and fear;
Suddenly the Lord, descending,
In His temple shall appear.
Come and worship, come and worship,
Worship Christ, the newborn King.

Sinners, wrung with true repentance,
Doomed for guilt to endless pains,
Justice now revokes the sentence,
Mercy calls you; break your chains.
Come and worship, come and worship,
Worship Christ, the newborn King.

Though an Infant now we view Him,
He shall fill His Father's throne,
Gather all the nations to Him;
Every knee shall then bow down:
Come and worship, come and worship,
Worship Christ, the newborn King.

All creation, join in praising
God, the Father, Spirit, Son,
Evermore your voices raising
To th'eternal Three in One.
Come and worship, come and worship,
Worship Christ, the newborn King.

Who?

James Montgomery was a Scots lad orphaned when his missionary parents died abroad. The Moravian church cared for him in Ireland before sending him to be educated in England.

A romantic, footloose soul, Montgomery dropped out of school, became a baker, a poet, a journalist, and eventually a newspaper owner. His concern for the poor and his social activism led to his being imprisoned twice.

What?

"Angels from the Realms of Glory" is a call to worship. It begins with the angels coming to proclaim the Messiah and includes a summons to sages and saints, whose work might be important, but not as important as worshipping the Lord.

Then, into this illustrious gathering, Montgomery calls the most important people of all—sinners! And he doesn't stop there. Not content with including sinners, which surely must mean every person on earth, Montgomery calls for all creation to join in the celebration.

Anyone keen to leave something behind after departing this life could hardly do better than did James Montgomery, whose call to worship the Lord is still remembered almost two hundred years later.

When?

First printed in 1816, which became known as "The Year without a Summer" after a volcanic explosion the year before, combined with unusually low solar activity, caused global temperatures to fall.

Also in 1816, Czar Alexander expelled Jesuits from the Russian Empire, and Indiana became the nineteenth U.S. state.

Where?

Montgomery's experience as a journalist in Yorkshire, England, enabled him to set up the *Sheffield Iris* newspaper, where "Angels from the Realms of Glory" was first published.

After a rootless childhood, Montgomery found a home in Sheffield. He is remembered there through a statue in the forecourt of Sheffield Cathedral.

Why?

James Montgomery had every reason to rebel against the Christian faith—after all, it could be said to have cost him his parents—and he did rebel in his teenage years. Later, however, the seeds of faith planted by his parents began to flower and brought him great comfort.

Montgomery achieved considerable success as a novelist and newspaperman, but when he was asked which of his works would outlive him, he replied, "None, sir! Except, perhaps, a few of my hymns." He probably wouldn't be disappointed to find that history has proved him right. In the end, as seen through his social activism and his hymn writing, his faith came to characterize his life.

OH COME, OH COME, EMMANUEL

Oh, come, oh, come, Emmanuel,
And ransom captive Israel,
That mourns in lonely exile here
Until the Son of God appear.
Rejoice! Rejoice! Emmanuel
Shall come to you, O Israel!

Oh, come, our Wisdom from on high,
Who ordered all things mightily;
To us the path of knowledge show,
And teach us in her ways to go.
Rejoice! Rejoice! Emmanuel
Shall come to you, O Israel!

Oh, come, oh, come, our Lord of might,
Who to your tribes on Sinai's height
In ancient times gave holy law,
In cloud and majesty and awe.
Rejoice! Rejoice! Emmanuel
Shall come to you, O Israel!

Oh, come, O Rod of Jesse's stem,
From ev'ry foe deliver them

That trust your mighty pow'r to save;
Bring them in vict'ry through the grave.
Rejoice! Rejoice! Emmanuel
Shall come to you, O Israel!

Oh, come, O Key of David, come,
And open wide our heav'nly home;
Make safe the way that leads on high,
And close the path to misery.
Rejoice! Rejoice! Emmanuel
Shall come to you, O Israel!

Oh, come, our Dayspring from on high,
And cheer us by your drawing nigh,
Disperse the gloomy clouds of night,
And death's dark shadows put to flight.
Rejoice! Rejoice! Emmanuel
Shall come to you, O Israel!

Oh, come, Desire of nations, bind
In one the hearts of all mankind;
Oh, bid our sad divisions cease,
And be yourself our King of Peace.
Rejoice! Rejoice! Emmanuel
Shall come to you, O Israel!

Who?

As the verses seem to have grown up with the church to become an established part of ancient church ritual, it will probably never be known who first put them together in the form of a song.

John Mason Neale, the warden of an English almshouse, played a major role in making Latin and Greek praise music available to English-speaking worshippers. Neale also wrote the carol "Good King Wenceslas," which is number twenty-six in our countdown.

What?

"Oh Come, Oh Come Emmanuel" is sung from the point of view of the exiled Jews, who have been humbled and taken into captivity because they deserted their God. If we were to look at their predicament in human terms, we might say that God is showing them what it feels like to be abandoned. He will come back. He will deliver them. But in his own time, and in His own way. Until then, the exiles can only cry for their homeland and long for their God.

The good news is that God has declared that He will never again abandon His people—and that includes everyone who trusts in Him. God is there for us when we need Him. "Oh Come,

Oh Come, Emmanuel" is a reminder of how blessed we are that Emmanuel has come.

When?

The verses that eventually became "Oh Come, Oh Come, Emmanuel" were written in the twelfth century, the same century in which the Crusades to the Holy Land began and reached their zenith. By the fifteenth century, these antiphons—verses sung responsively as part of a liturgy—had been arranged into the processional hymn "Veni, Veni Emanuel." In the late nineteenth century, the verses were translated from Latin to English and became the carol we know today.

Where?

The Latin chants on which this song was based were first sung by monks in French medieval monasteries. They might have been pleased to know that their song would still be sung eight centuries later.

Why?

The original verses were a series of responses based on the names of Jesus, usually sung the week before Christmas. They were called the "O antiphons" and referred to Christ as Wisdom,

Adonai, Root of Jesse, Key of David, Dayspring, King of Nations, and Emmanuel. By taking the first letter of each of these names in Latin and arranging them in reverse order, the monks could spell *"Ero Cras,"* which means, "Tomorrow, I will come."

31 · THE VIRGIN MARY HAD A BABY BOY

The virgin Mary had a baby boy,
The virgin Mary had a baby boy,
The virgin Mary had a baby boy,
And they say that his name is Jesus.

Chorus
He come from the glory,
He come from the glorious kingdom.
He come from the glory,
He come from the glorious kingdom.
Oh, yes! believer! Oh, yes! believer!
He come from the glory,
He come from the glorious kingdom.

The angels sang when the baby was born,
The angels sang when the baby was born,
The angels sang when the baby was born,

And they say that his name is Jesus.

Chorus

The shepherds came where the baby was born,
The shepherds came where the baby was born,
The shepherds came where the baby was born,
And they say that his name is Jesus.

Chorus

The Wise Men came where the baby was born,
The Wise Men came where the baby was born,
The Wise Men came where the baby was born,
And they say that his name is Jesus.

Who?

Spanish missionaries brought the concept of the Immaculate Conception to the inhabitants of the West Indies. The native populations, many of whom were enslaved, may have incorporated the miracle into their work songs.

Edric Connor was a Trinidadian who moved to London and made a successful career out of singing traditional calypso songs.

What?

"The Virgin Mary Had a Baby Boy" is a simple rhythmic song, one that might easily be picked up after a single hearing. It is endlessly repeat-able and endlessly adaptable, as long as the sing-ers stick to the one miraculous central truth—that Christ was born of a virgin!

When?

This song may have originated as far back as the sixteenth century when Spain was colonizing the West Indies. Possibly published for the first time by Edric Connor in 1945.

Where?

Spanish West Indian colonies.

Why?

The Spanish missionaries wanted all the king's subjects to know about Jesus. They saw it as their duty to "civilize" and save as many people as they could.

The plantation workers who first sang the song probably drew strength from the knowl-edge that there was something altogether more wonderful in store for them after the short, hard lives they were living.

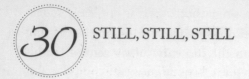

30 STILL, STILL, STILL

Still, still, still
One can hear the falling snow.
For all is hushed,
The world is sleeping,
Holy Star its vigil keeping.
Still, still, still,
One can hear the falling snow.

Sleep, sleep, sleep,
'Tis the eve of our Saviour's birth.
The night is peaceful all around you,
Close your eyes,
Let sleep surround you.
Sleep, sleep, sleep
'Tis the eve of our Saviour's birth.

Dream, dream, dream,
Of the joyous day to come.
While guardian angels without
Watch you as you sweetly slumber.
Dream, dream, dream,
Of the joyous day to come.

Who?

"Still, Still, Still" is a carol that seems to have sprung straight from the hearts of the people. There may have been an original composer, but his or her name is lost to the ages. The song has passed through the generations but still preserves the same sense of peace and comfort.

What?

"Still, Still, Still" is a soothing lullaby with a gently repetitive lyric that contains the promise of "joyous days to come." It's the promise most loving parents make to their children; the same one God made to the world when He sent us Jesus.

When?

"Still, Still, Still" was written in 1819, the same year the U.S. suffered its first major financial crisis; and Spain gave up all claims to Florida.

Where?

In the mountains of Austria.

Why?

Before paved roads and automobiles, the Austrians didn't travel any more than was necessary in the middle of winter. There probably would have

been a real sense of settling down and waiting
waiting for better things to come.

The world, had it known of the Savior's im-
pending birth, probably would have had a simi-
lar sense of anticipation.

 THE COVENTRY CAROL

Lullay, Thou little tiny Child,
By, by, lully, lullay.
Lullay, Thou little tiny Child.
By, by, lully, lullay.

O sisters, too, how may we do,
For to preserve this day;
This poor Youngling for whom we sing,
By, by, lully, lullay.

Herod the King, in his raging,
Charged he hath this day;
His men of might, in his own sight,
All children young, to slay.

Then woe is me, poor Child, for Thee,
And ever mourn and say;

For Thy parting, nor say nor sing,
By, by, lully, lullay.

Who?

Robert Croo provided the earliest recorded text of the carol, though it certainly existed before he transcribed it. Croo was a member of the Cappers guild who also became involved in the theater as a pageant master and translator of texts.

What?

"The Coventry Carol," which undoubtedly had a different name when it was first written, was one of at least three songs from *The Pageant of the Shearmen and Tailors,* but the only one to survive the ravages of time.

The carol is a reminder that, though we celebrate the birth of Christ, many mothers wept on that first Nativity. Their children had fallen victim to Herod's hunt for the Christ child.

In the play, the song occurs as the mothers try to soothe their children in the forlorn hope that the soldiers will pass them by. The "lully lullay" used to calm the children to sleep may be the source of our word *lullaby.*

The haunting tones of "The Coventry Carol" remind us that the first Christmas, though a time of great joy, was bought at a price and is all the more precious because of it.

When?

The oldest existing copy of this carol dates back to 1534. In that same year, King Henry VIII created the Church of England after the pope refused to grant him a divorce; Martin Luther completed his German translation of the Bible; and Jacques Cartier became the first European to travel up the St. Lawrence River.

Where?

The city of Coventry, England, has a long history of mystery plays. These were staged Nativity plays that tried to portray the miracle and mystery of the Incarnation.

In the sixteenth century (and before), tradesmen's and merchants' guilds performed these plays on carts or platforms in the streets, during the weeks leading up to Christmas.

Why?

The texts to the mystery plays were closely guarded by the city. Each city tried to outdo the others, because having a famous play performed in the streets was an early form of tourist attraction.

More visitors meant more money into the city's treasury.

Not everyone was allowed to see, let alone copy, the texts, and those lucky enough to get such access had to pay for the privilege. Robert Croo, as a man of distinction in Coventry, was permitted the honor. His transcribed text was lost in a fire at the Birmingham Library in 1879; but by then copies of his copy had been made.

 ## 28 I SAW THREE SHIPS

I saw three ships come sailing in,
On Christmas day, on Christmas day,
I saw three ships come sailing in,
On Christmas day in the morning.

And what was in those ships all three?
On Christmas day, on Christmas day,
And what was in those ships all three?
On Christmas day in the morning.

Our Saviour Christ and his lady
On Christmas day, on Christmas day,
Our Saviour Christ and his lady,
On Christmas day in the morning.

Pray whither sailed those ships all three?
On Christmas day, on Christmas day,
Pray whither sailed those ships all three?
On Christmas day in the morning.

Oh, they sailed into Bethlehem,
On Christmas day, on Christmas day,
Oh, they sailed into Bethlehem,
On Christmas day in the morning.

And all the bells on earth shall ring,
On Christmas day, on Christmas day,
And all the bells on earth shall ring,
On Christmas day in the morning.

And all the Angels in Heaven shall sing,
On Christmas day, on Christmas day,
And all the Angels in Heaven shall sing,
On Christmas day in the morning.

And all the souls on earth shall sing,
On Christmas day, on Christmas day,
And all the souls on earth shall sing,
On Christmas day in the morning.

Then let us all rejoice, amain,
On Christmas day, on Christmas day,
Then let us all rejoice, amain,
On Christmas day in the morning.

Who?

It is unknown who composed this very popular carol, but the earliest known version appears in *Cantus, Songs and Fancies* by John Forbes, who was associated with the University of Aberdeen in Scotland.

The song is often sung to the alternative tune *Greensleeves*, which popular legend attributes to King Henry VIII as composer.

What?

"I Saw Three Ships" may have once had a deep, symbolic meaning that has been lost over the ages. To most carolers, though, it is a catchy, easy to sing, almost nonsensical song, but one which nonetheless has brought joy to many carolers and listeners.

The magi who may have sailed in those original ships—either themselves or in relic form—have been replaced in the song over time by various groupings of the Holy Family who are harping, whistling, singing, or otherwise celebrating Christ's arrival. And the magi's destination has changed from Cologne, Germany, to the scene of their most famous visit—Bethlehem.

Ships could never sail to Bethlehem, which is miles from the Mediterranean, or even from the landlocked Sea of Galilee. But even though the lyrics don't seem to make much sense, the carol remains a firm favorite with all ages. And who knows? With Jesus at the helm of the ship…well…anything's possible!

When?

This carol was first printed in 1666, the same year that an accident in a baker's house started the Great Fire of London, which burned for three days and nights, consuming four-fifths of the walled city.

Also in 1666, Sir Isaac Newton split light into its component colors using a prism, and the city of Newark was founded by Connecticut Puritans.

Where?

Early versions of the carol can be found in counties the length and breadth of England, though an old Scottish verse may well have a claim to being the prototype.

Why?

Many early versions have the singer sitting under a tree, or by his cottage door, and looking out to sea. Across the glistening waves he sees three ships.

In the modern version, the singer sees "Christ and His lady," presumably a reference to Jesus' mother, Mary. In earlier versions, each ship carried one of the three wise men. This may refer to a time in the twelfth century when three ships supposedly brought relics of the magi to Germany.

Someone sitting on the south coast of England (with a strong telescope) may well have seen ships bound for Germany sailing up the English Channel.

 ## 27 HE IS BORN, THE DIVINE CHRIST CHILD

Chorus
He is born, the divine Christ child.
Play on the oboe and bagpipes merrily.
He is born, the divine Christ child.
Sing we all of the Saviour's birth.

Through long ages of the past,
Prophets have foretold his coming;
Through long ages of the past,
Now the time has come at last.

Chorus

Oh, how lovely, oh, how pure.
Is this perfect child of heaven.

Oh, how lovely, oh, how pure,
Gracious gift of God, to man.

Chorus

Jesus, Lord of all the world,
Coming as a child among us,
Jesus, Lord of all the world,
Grant to us Thy heav'nly peace.

Chorus

Who?

Although Dom G. Legeay published the carol in 1875, he gave no clue as to the author. As the carol may already have been one hundred years old, it's likely he didn't know.

The first recorded version of the melody was published in 1862 by R. Grossjean.

What?

This carol has been described as an "eighteenth century piece in the rustic style," which might be a polite way of describing the enthusiasm with which it is sometimes played.

The hymn is sung in different tempos, with varying lyrics and a variety of instruments, all across the world. There is even a version sung by Native Americans in their own language.

Whether it is sung as "Il Est Ne, Le Divin Enfant," or "He Is Born, the Divine Christ Child," or the Mohawk version, "Rotonni Niio Roie Mia," the heart of the piece is one of rejoicing that Christ was born for us. The number of different versions reflects the variety of the people who sing it.

So, grab your bagpipes, oboes, pipes, and drums, or whatever your instrument of choice is, and make a joyous noise—because the divine Christ child is born for everyone!

When?

"He Is Born, the Divine Christ Child" is a traditional French carol first published in 1875, the year Tufts and Harvard played what was arguably the first game of college football. That same year, Albert Schweitzer, the renowned doctor, musician, and missionary was born. The Civil Rights Act of 1875 guaranteed people of any color the same treatment in public accommodations, but was later declared unconstitutional.

Where?

"He Is Born, the Divine Christ Child" is one of many translations of the French carol "Il Est Ne, Le Divin Enfant." The melody, first published in *Airs des Noëls Lorrain*, is believed to have been based on an old hunting song, or *"ancien air de chasse,"* from Normandy.

Why?

Everyone likes a celebration. "He Is Born, the Divine Christ Child" shows that the French villagers thought the birth of Jesus was an event worth celebrating, and worth celebrating with enthusiasm and a lot of noise. Instruments to play "merrily" in the many variations of the song include the oboe, musette, trumpets, drums, and bagpipes.

The villagers must have felt entitled to a good old party, because according to two different versions of the song, they had been waiting for Christ's birth "through long ages of the past," or for "four thousand years."

GOOD KING WENCESLAS

Good King Wenceslas looked out
On the feast of Stephen,
When the snow lay round about,
Deep and crisp and even,
Brightly shone the moon that night,
Though the frost was cruel,
When a poor man came in sight,
Gath'ring winter fuel.

"Hither, page, and stand by me.
If thou know'st it, telling
Yonder peasant, who is he?
Where and what his dwelling?"
"Sire, he lives a good league hence
Underneath the mountain,
Right against the forest fence
By Saint Agnes' fountain."

"Bring me flesh and bring me wine.
Bring me pine logs hither.
Thou and I will see him dine
When we bear him thither."
Page and monarch forth they went,

Forth they went together
Through the rude wind's wild lament
And the bitter weather.

"Sire, the night is darker now
And the wind blows stronger.
Fails my heart, I know not how,
I can go no longer."
"Mark my footsteps, my good page
Tread thou in them boldly.
Thou shalt find the winter's rage
Freeze thy blood less coldly."

In his master's steps he trod
Where the snow lay dinted.
Heat was in the very sod
Which the Saint had printed
Therefore, Christian men, be sure,
Wealth or rank possessing
Ye who now will bless the poor
Shall yourselves find blessing.

Who?

John Mason Neale was ordained in 1841, but
poor health prevented him taking up a parish
for five years. While traveling for his health, he

first read the legend of Svaty Vaclav, duke of Bohemia, also known as Wenceslas.

Neale was a translator of Latin and Greek hymns. "Good King Wenceslas" is thought to be an original work, but it may have been a translation of an earlier Wenceslas poem by the Czech poet Vaclav Alois Svoboda, who wrote under the pen name of Navarovsky.

What?

Good King Wenceslas was a real historical figure. He wasn't actually a king (that honor was bestowed posthumously), but by most accounts he was certainly good.

Th ts out, barefoot and with a single page (named Otto), to bring food and firewood to a poor family. Otto suffers greatly from the cold and insists his heart is about to fail. Wenceslas advises Otto to follow in his footsteps, and the page finds warmth emanating from his lord's footsteps.

The song ends by saying that, no matter whether you are a duke or a poor man, the surest way to be blessed is to be a blessing to others. Isn't that a message worth remembering at Christmas?

When?

The first appearance of "Good King Wenceslas" as a carol came in 1853, the same year that missionary Hudson Taylor left for China; Franklin Pierce became the fourteenth U.S. president; and potato chips were invented.

Where?

Neale may have come across the legend of Wenceslas while traveling abroad, but it was while settled back in England that he included the duke's story in the book *Deeds of Faith,* which he dedicated to his daughter, Agnes.

Why?

Neale had a passionate interest in the history of the church, its architecture, its music, and its saints. Compiling a book of "deeds of faith" for his daughter to read, he could hardly resist including the story of Wenceslas, even though he wasn't sure if it was absolutely true.

"Supposing it a legend," he writes, "it is a legend of such extreme beauty that it may well find a place in a series of tales like the present."

SILENT NIGHT

Silent night, holy night,
All is calm, all is bright
Round yon virgin mother and Child.
Holy Infant, so tender and mild,
Sleep in heavenly peace,
Sleep in heavenly peace.

Silent night, holy night,
Shepherds quake at the sight;
Glories stream from heaven afar,
Heavenly hosts sing Alleluia!
Christ the Savior is born,
Christ the Savior is born!

Silent night, holy night,
Son of God, love's pure light;
Radiant beams from Thy holy face
With the dawn of redeeming grace,
Jesus, Lord, at Thy birth,
Jesus, Lord, at Thy birth
Silent night, holy night
Wondrous star, lend thy light;
With the angels let us sing,

Alleluia to our King;
Christ the Savior is born,
Christ the Savior is born!

Who?

Josef Franz Mohr had an unfortunate start to life. His soldier father deserted both the army and his seamstress wife before Mohr was born.

Mohr's rare musical ability encouraged a patron to sponsor his religious education, but having been born illegitimately, Mohr required a special papal dispensation to allow him into the priesthood.

The original tune was written by Mohr's friend Franz Gruber. The English translation of the carol, by John Freeman Young in 1819, softened the melody, which was originally more upbeat.

What?

"Silent Night" has a sense of the world holding its breath, waiting for something truly momentous. It may refer to some of the Apocryphal Gospels, which suggest the world actually fell silent and nature stood still in anticipation of the birth of Jesus.

From Mohr's very own silent night, when the organ broke down, his song has gone on to fill the silence with worship and adoration on

Christmas Eves for the better part of two centuries—and in at least forty-five languages.

When?

In 1816, when the poem "Stille Nacht" was written, James Monroe was elected the fifth president of the United States; Indiana became the nineteenth state; the Gas Light Company of Baltimore was founded; and the Bonaparte family was expelled from France.

Where?

The Church of St. Nicholas in Oberndorf, Austria, was the setting for the first performance of "Silent Night" in 1818, but the text was written two years earlier, while Mohr worked at a pilgrim church in Mariapfarr, Austria.

Why?

The traditional version of the "Silent Night" story has mice eating through the cables of the church organ. The poor priest then has to come up with a Christmas Eve hymn that can be performed without the dilapidated old instrument.

The truth was a little more harsh, but no less wonderful. Mohr assisted a liberal senior priest who believed in translating services and hymns into the language of his parishioners. Unfortunately, the church insisted that everything be in Latin. Mohr's priest was then replaced by a hard-liner who held Mohr's illegitimate birth against him.

The church organ did die on Christmas Eve, but whether mice were responsible is not known. Mohr took a poem he had written to his friend headmaster Franz Gruber, and together they came up with a song that could be accompanied by a guitar.

Instead of the usual Latin hymns, "Silent Night" was sung in German, the language of Mohr's parishioners.

24 GO TELL IT ON THE MOUNTAIN

Chorus
Go, tell it on the mountain,
Over the hills and everywhere
Go, tell it on the mountain,
That Jesus Christ is born.

While shepherds kept their watching
Over silent flocks by night
Behold throughout the heavens
There shone a holy light.

Chorus

The shepherds feared and trembled,
When lo! above the earth,
Rang out the angels' chorus
That hailed the Savior's birth.

Chorus

Down in a lowly manger
The humble Christ was born
And God sent us salvation
That blessed Christmas morn.

Who?

John Wesley Work Jr. was born in Nashville in 1871. He is believed to have been the first African American collector of songs sung by American slaves.

What?

"Go Tell It on the Mountain" is a simple retelling of the Nativity, punctuated by exhortations to go tell the Good News on the mountains, overseas, and to every corner of the world.

People suffering intolerable conditions clung to that Good News, and they told it to their children. Along the way, someone told it to John Wesley Work Jr., and he told the world. Now, who are *you* going to tell?

When?

The song was passed down by tradition, and was published for the first time in 1907, the same year that Guglielmo Marconi initiated a transatlantic radio service; and Hershey's Kisses were introduced.

Where?

Work published several collections of music while living in Nashville, including *New Jubilee Songs* and *Folk Songs of the American Negro*.

"Go Tell It on the Mountain" was published in 1907, independent of any collection.

Why?

Fisk University, where Work was taught and went on to teach, grew from the Fisk Free Colored School, set up to educate freed slaves and their children. It would have already been steeped in slave folklore when Work enrolled.

23 ANGELS WE HAVE HEARD ON HIGH

Angels we have heard on high
Sweetly singing o'er the plains,
And the mountains in reply
Echoing their joyous strains.

Chorus
Gloria, in excelsis Deo!
Gloria, in excelsis Deo!

Shepherds, why this jubilee?
Why your joyous strains prolong?
What the gladsome tidings be
Which inspire your heavenly song?

Chorus

Come to Bethlehem and see
Him whose birth the angels sing;
Come, adore on bended knee,
Christ the Lord, the newborn King.

Chorus

See Him in a manger laid,
Whom the choirs of angels praise;
Mary, Joseph, lend your aid,
While our hearts in love we raise.

Chorus

Who?

The creators of the original versions of this hymn are unknown, but they may actually have been shepherds, echoing the place of honor their Jewish counterparts occupied at the first Nativity.

It was translated into English by James Chadwick, at the time a professor of pastoral theology at Usher College.

The music, commonly known as "Gloria," was composed by Edward Shippen Barnes, the organist at the Church of the Incarnation in New York City.

What?

The shepherds may have expanded on the "Gloria in excelsis" as they walked the hills, or the rest of the lyrics may have been from an earlier traditional carol, but at some point, the two joined together to create "Les Anges dans nos Campagnes" or "The Angels in Our Fields."

The shepherds in the song are making a glorious noise and inviting everyone to come and see what all the fuss is about. The "fuss," of course, was the birth of Jesus Christ.

The angels proclaimed Christ's arrival two thousand years ago, and the shepherds carried on the tradition; but now it's our turn to celebrate. Let's sing in such a way that we will be heard even by those angels on high!

When?

"Angels We Have Heard on High" is a traditional song, parts of which are thought to date from the eighteenth century; but the completed version was translated into English in 1860. That same year, the Pony Express began its first mail service, riding from Missouri to California; the world's earliest sound recording was made; and Abraham Lincoln became the sixteenth president of the United States.

Where?

The roots of "Angels We Have Heard on High" are firmly planted in the hillsides of Lorraine in France. It was translated into Cornish and Scottish Gaelic and became almost traditional in both locales.

James Chadwick, the English translator, was bishop of Hexham and Newcastle. He published the carol in his collection *Holy Family Hymns* in 1860. The first French version was published in Quebec eighteen years earlier.

Why?

According to popular legend, shepherds on the French hillsides in the weeks before Christmas sang "Gloria in excelsis" to each other across the valleys. It was a way of affirming their piety, echoing the song the angels had sung to the shepherds at the first Nativity, and not getting lost. If you could hear a fellow worker singing nearby, you knew you hadn't strayed too far in the dark of the evening.

22 WE THREE KINGS OF ORIENT ARE

We three kings of Orient are;
Bearing gifts we traverse afar,
Field and fountain, moor and mountain,
Following yonder star.

Chorus
O star of wonder, star of light,
Star with royal beauty bright,
Westward leading, still proceeding,
Guide us to thy perfect light.

Born a King on Bethlehem's plain
Gold I bring to crown Him again,
King forever, ceasing never,
Over us all to reign.

Chorus
Frankincense to offer have I;
Incense owns a Deity nigh;
Prayer and praising, voices raising,
Worshipping God on high.

Chorus

Myrrh is mine, its bitter perfume
Breathes a life of gathering gloom;
Sorrowing, sighing, bleeding, dying,
Sealed in the stone cold tomb.

Chorus

Glorious now behold Him arise;
King and God and sacrifice;
Alleluia, Alleluia,
Sounds through the earth and skies.

Chorus

Who?

John Henry Hopkins Jr. was the son of a bishop of Vermont. On course to become a lawyer, he instead entered General Theological Seminary and eventually became the school's first music teacher. Eventually he became the rector of Christ Church in Williamsport, Pennsylvania.

Hopkins published two books of music, and his other compositions include "Gather Round the Christmas Tree" and "Alleluia! Christ Is Risen Today!"

He also delivered the eulogy for President Ulysses S. Grant.

What?

No one knows how many kings, wise men, or magi were actually present at the birth of Christ. It has long been believed there was one king for each of the gifts, and Hopkins's jaunty carol may have played a large part in perpetuating the myth. Nevertheless, the song is full of devotion, describing the journey the three kings made "from afar" to acknowledge the baby Jesus as "King and God and sacrifice."

Hopkins's song is about gifts, both the gifts the magi gave and the gift that the Son of God was. His song was a gift to his colleagues and the family's children in 1857. It has been a wonderful gift to the world ever since.

When?

"We Three Kings of Orient Are" was written in 1857. In that same year, the British East India Company was fighting the Sepoy Rebellion in India. Karl Marx published an article in the *New-York Daily Tribune* denouncing the British.

Also in 1857, America celebrated the linking of Baltimore with St. Louis by rail, and construction began on a transatlantic cable.

Where?

The carol first appeared in print in 1863 in Hopkins's own collection, *Carols, Hymns, and Songs.* Two years later, its increased fame merited a special illustrated publication of its own. It may have been written at the seminary in New York, and it was performed at a Christmas pageant there.

Why?

Hopkins was a very family oriented man. Having no children of his own, he looked forward to treating his nieces and nephews. The children anticipated family gatherings, certain that Uncle John (who later became known as Vermont's Father Christmas) would have some delight in store for them.

At Christmas in 1857, their treat was a new song to sing, "We Three Kings of Orient Are." In a day when most entertainment was homemade, a new song would have been a delightful surprise.

21 O LITTLE TOWN OF BETHLEHEM

O little town of Bethlehem, how still we see thee lie!
Above thy deep and dreamless sleep the silent stars
go by.
Yet in thy dark streets shineth the everlasting Light;
The hopes and fears of all the years are met in thee
tonight.

For Christ is born of Mary, and gathered all above,
While mortals sleep, the angels keep their watch of
wondering love.
O morning stars together, proclaim the holy birth,
And praises sing to God the King, and peace to men
on earth!

How silently, how silently, the wondrous Gift is giv'n;
So God imparts to human hearts the blessings of
His Heav'n.
No ear may hear His coming, but in this world of sin,
Where meek souls will receive Him still, the dear
Christ enters in.

Where children pure and happy pray to the blessed
Child,
Where misery cries out to Thee, Son of the mother mild;

*Where charity stands watching and faith holds
    wide the door,
The dark night wakes, the glory breaks, and Christmas
    comes once more.*

*O holy Child of Bethlehem, descend to us, we pray;
Cast out our sin, and enter in, be born in us today.
We hear the Christmas angels the great glad tidings tell;
O come to us, abide with us, our Lord Emmanuel!*

Who?

Phillips Brooks became known by many as the greatest American preacher of the nineteenth century. Born in Massachusetts, he attended Harvard University, where the Phillips Brooks House bears his name. A supporter of the abolition of slavery, Brooks also campaigned for the right of freed slaves to vote. He later became the Episcopal bishop of Massachusetts.

Lewis H. Redner, who composed the music, was a real estate broker who played the organ at Holy Trinity Episcopal Church in Philadelphia while Brooks was rector there. Popular legend has it that the melody came to Redner on Christmas Eve and was first performed on Christmas Day.

What?

After his visit to the town, Brooks wrote "O Little Town of Bethlehem" as "a simple little carol for the church Sunday school Christmas service." So it was sung and so it has continued to be sung. The carol has a good claim to being the first Christmas carol most children learn.

The song addresses the very adult themes of sin and redemption, but Brooks may have had in mind Jesus' advice that we "become as little children" when he wrote the lyrics. He speaks of "meek souls" receiving Him, and "children pure and happy" praying.

Bethlehem, like the rest of the world, has changed; but as Brooks realized while watching that sleeping town, wherever a willing heart invites Jesus in, sins will be cast out, and we can all be as children again in the house of our Father.

When?

The carol was written in 1867, from notes written two years before. Also in 1867, the United States demanded the removal of French forces from Mexico; Peru declared war on Spain; and the American Equal Rights Society and the American Society for the Prevention of Cruelty to Animals were both constituted.

Where?

The notes that eventually became the carol were written as Brooks was camped in the hills of Palestine at night, looking down onto the town of Bethlehem. He completed his journey and helped officiate at a service in Bethlehem on Christmas Eve 1865.

Why?

Sitting in the Palestinian hills, looking down at the birthplace of his Savior, must have had a powerful effect on Phillips Brooks. The landscape and town and the lifestyles of the people would not have been so greatly different from when Jesus was born there.

THE HOLLY AND THE IVY

The holly and the ivy, now both are full well grown.
Of all the trees that are in the wood, the holly bears
*   the crown.*

Chorus

Oh, the rising of the sun, the running of the deer.
The playing of the merry organ, sweet singing in
*   the choir.*

The holly bears a blossom as white as lily flower;
And Mary bore sweet Jesus Christ to be our sweet
*   Savior.*

Chorus

The holly bears a berry as red as any blood;
And Mary bore sweet Jesus Christ to do poor
*   sinners good.*

Chorus

The holly bears a prickle as sharp as any thorn;
And Mary bore sweet Jesus Christ on Christmas
*   day in the morn.*

Chorus

The holly bears a bark as bitter as any gall;
And Mary bore sweet Jesus Christ for to redeem us all.

Chorus

The holly and the ivy, when they are both full grown,
Of all the trees that are in the wood, the holly bears
the crown.

Chorus

Who?

In all probability, the original authors of the song were medieval British Christians.

Much later, the Reverend Henry Bramley and Sir John Stainer published their three-volume *Christmas Carols, New and Old,* which preserved many older, traditional carols. "The Holly and the Ivy" appeared in the second volume.

What?

The carol we know today as "The Holly and the Ivy" was written around another, older song, "The Contest between the Holly and the Ivy."

In the "contest," holly represents the masculine and ivy is feminine. The holly is master of his warm, comfortable house, while the ivy hangs about the door wishing she were inside.

This surely is another theme the monks would have had no difficulty in adapting. After all, Jesus is the Son of Man and the house we desperately want into is heaven.

The battle between male and female might still go on today, but any man who thinks he has won it is only fooling himself. The crown of holly the victor wears represents the crown of thorns, and the red berries are the blood that was shed for the saving of all mankind.

As we sing joyfully at Christmastime, may it be that the true master of our homes is neither the holly nor the ivy—the man nor the woman—but only the Son of Man!

When?

This traditional carol was first published in 1871 (though it was mentioned in print 160 years earlier and is undoubtedly centuries older than that). In 1871 Prussian troops bombarded Paris in the Franco-Prussian War; the U.S. Congress passed the Indian Appropriation Act, giving the government authority over Native American affairs; and "Wild Bill" Hickok became marshal of Abilene, Kansas.

Where?

The oldest known versions of "The Holly and the Ivy" come from the southern counties of England, where there was traditionally a strong Druidic influence. Today, the carol is sung all over the English-speaking world.

Why?

In medieval times, holly and ivy were used to decorate churches at Christmastime. It's likely, however, that the Christian monks were borrowing from an older pagan belief, and perhaps trying to assimilate the two.

Druids had long used the two plants for healing—and because both holly and ivy are evergreens, they were seen as a symbol of life in the midst of the dark winter. The monks would surely have had no problem in relating these same properties to Jesus Christ.

THE TWELVE DAYS OF CHRISTMAS

On the first day of Christmas, my true love sent to me: a partridge in a pear tree.

On the second day of Christmas, my true love sent to me: two turtledoves, and a partridge in a pear tree.

On the third day of Christmas, my true love sent to me: three French hens, two turtledoves, and a partridge in a pear tree.

On the fourth day of Christmas, my true love sent to me: four calling birds, three French hens, two turtledoves, and a partridge in a pear tree.

On the fifth day of Christmas, my true love sent to me: five golden rings, four calling birds, three French hens, two turtledoves, and a partridge in a pear tree.

On the sixth day of Christmas, my true love sent to me: six geese a-laying, five golden rings, four calling birds, three French hens, two turtledoves, and a partridge in a pear tree.

On the seventh day of Christmas, my true love sent to me: seven swans a-swimming, six geese a-laying, five golden rings, four calling birds, three French hens, two turtledoves, and a partridge in a pear tree.

On the eighth day of Christmas, my true love sent to me: eight maids a-milking, seven swans a-swimming, six geese a-laying, five golden rings, four calling birds, three French hens, two turtle-doves, and a partridge in a pear tree.

On the ninth day of Christmas, my true love sent to me: nine ladies dancing, eight maids a-milking, seven swans a-swimming, six geese a-laying, five golden rings, four calling birds, three French hens, two turtledoves, and a partridge in a pear tree.

On the tenth day of Christmas, my true love sent to me: ten lords a-leaping, nine ladies dancing, eight maids a-milking, seven swans a-swimming, six geese a-laying, five golden rings, four calling birds, three French hens, two turtledoves, and a partridge in a pear tree.

On the eleventh day of Christmas, my true love sent to me: eleven pipers piping, ten lords a-leaping, nine ladies dancing, eight maids a-milking, seven swans a-swimming, six geese a-laying, five golden rings, four calling birds, three French hens, two turtle-doves, and a partridge in a pear tree.

On the twelfth day of Christmas, my true love sent to me: twelve drummers drumming, eleven pipers piping, ten lords a-leaping, nine ladies dancing, eight maids a-milking, seven swans a-swimming, six geese a-laying, five golden rings, four calling birds, three French hens, two turtledoves, and a partridge in a pear tree.

Who?

No one knows who wrote "The Twelve Days of Christmas," but its association with Twelfth Night parties and certain textual clues indicate the authors were most likely French Christians.

What?

Many and various are the theories behind the obscure gifts given in "The Twelve Days of Christmas." Perhaps the most widely held "conspiracy theory" is that the Catholic Church used it as a "catechism code" in England after the Reformation.

In one account, the "true love" was God and His gifts were things such as the Gospels (the four calling birds) and the Old and New Testaments (two turtledoves).

In times gone by, it was also claimed that the relationship between particular gifts and the days they belonged to would accurately forecast the weather for the year ahead.

In the final analysis, "The Twelve Days of Christmas" probably has little or no spiritual content. It is probably just a happy party song originally sung by people who had spent the Christmas period sincerely worshipping their Lord and were now having a little fun.

Fun at Christmastime? Surely that's a gift of an idea!

When?

First published in 1846 from an "oral tradition," so the song is obviously much older. In its year of the carol's publication, the Liberty Bell cracked; California declared independence from Mexico; the planet Neptune was discovered by German astronomers; and "Buffalo Bill" Cody was born.

Where?

Although the carol is firmly established as traditionally English, its earliest variations were probably sung in France. It's still sung there under the title "La foi de la loi," which differs from the English version in many of its gifts (for example, "full-breasted maidens" and "musketeers with their swords").

Why?

In many traditions, Christmas Day was a solemn, prayer-filled occasion. Gift giving would begin on Boxing Day and continue until Twelfth Night, when the major party of the season would be held. As part of the entertainment at these parties (and with a considerable degree of showing off), people would be challenged to recite all the gifts they had received.

In a spirit of fun, perhaps fueled by too much wine, the gifts often included imaginary and outrageous items. The singer of the Scottish version claims to have been given an "Arabian baboon" by her true love!

The song was very much in the style of memory/forfeit games popular at such parties. So, rather than forfeit one's turn, plenty of imagination would be employed.

18 HARK! THE HERALD ANGELS SING

Hark! The herald angels sing,
"Glory to the newborn King;
Peace on earth, and mercy mild,
God and sinners reconciled!"
Joyful, all ye nations rise,
Join the triumph of the skies;
With th'angelic host proclaim,
"Christ is born in Bethlehem!"

Chorus
Hark! the herald angels sing,
"Glory to the newborn King!"

Christ, by highest Heav'n adored;
Christ the everlasting Lord;
Late in time, behold Him come,
Offspring of a Virgin's womb.
Veiled in flesh the Godhead see;
Hail th'incarnate Deity,
Pleased as man with man to dwell,
Jesus our Emmanuel.
Chorus

Hail the heav'n-born Prince of Peace!
Hail the Sun of Righteousness!
Light and life to all He brings,
Ris'n with healing in His wings.
Mild He lays His glory by,
Born that man no more may die.
Born to raise the sons of earth,
Born to give them second birth.

Chorus

Come, Desire of nations, come,
Fix in us Thy humble home;
Rise, the woman's conqu'ring Seed,
Bruise in us the serpent's head.
Now display Thy saving power,
Ruined nature now restore;
Now in mystic union join
Thine to ours, and ours to Thine.

Chorus

Adam's likeness, Lord, efface,
Stamp Thine image in its place:
Second Adam from above,
Reinstate us in Thy love.
Let us Thee, though lost, regain,
Thee, the Life, the inner man:
O, to all Thyself impart,
Formed in each believing heart.

Who?

Charles Wesley was the brother of John Wesley, founder of the Methodist movement. Unlike his brother, Charles was against splitting with the Church of England and specifically requested that he be buried by the Church of England when he died.

He is best remembered for the thousands of hymns he composed, including "Hark! The Herald Angels Sing," "Jesus, Lover of My Soul," and "Christ the Lord Is Risen Today."

The music for "Hark! The Herald Angels Sing" is from a cantata composed by Felix Mendelssohn to celebrate the invention of the printing press.

What?

In his original version, Wesley's first line was "Hark! how all the welkin rings, glory to the King of kings." The word *welkin* has largely fallen out of use these days, but in Wesley's time it meant the celestial sphere, where the angels lived, everything heavenly. *All* of that, he insisted, must have rejoiced at the birth of Christ!

In 1872 "Hark! The Herald Angels Sing" was included as one of "the four great Anglican hymns" in the 1872 publication *The Church Hymn*

Book. Two of those four hymns came from the pen of Charles Wesley, with the other one being "Lo, He Comes with Clouds Descending."

The herald angels may well have sung at the birth of Jesus, but with more than 6,500 hymns to his name, Charles Wesley certainly did his best to keep the rest of us singing about that wonderful event.

When?

"Hark! The Herald Angels Sing" was written in 1739, the same year that Great Britain declared war on Spain in the War of Jenkins's Ear; the Stono Slave Rebellion took place in South Carolina; and Dick Turpin, the English highwayman, was hanged.

Where?

Wesley published "Hark! The Herald Angels Sing" in his collection *Hymns and Sacred Poems*.

The Wesley brothers had spent a few years traveling in the New World. On their return to Britain, they formed a group with other preachers and traveled around their homeland. It was during this time in England that Charles Wesley wrote "Hark! The Herald Angels Sing."

Why?

Popular legend says that Wesley heard the church bells ringing on Christmas Eve and felt compelled to write the words that, after changes by George Whitefield and several others, became "Hark! The Herald Angels Sing."

Being of sober character, Wesley had his carol sung to a slow melody. A hundred years later, it was paired with Mendelssohn's music to make an altogether more joyful sound.

17 CAROL OF THE BELLS

Hark! how the bells
Sweet silver bells
All seem to say,
"Throw cares away."
Christmas is here
Bringing good cheer
To young and old
Meek and the bold.

Ding, dong, ding, dong
That is their song
With joyful ring

All caroling
One seems to hear
Words of good cheer
From ev'rywhere
Filling the air.

Oh how they pound,
Raising the sound,
O'er hill and dale,
Telling their tale,
Gaily they ring
While people sing
Songs of good cheer
Christmas is here
Merry, merry, merry, merry Christmas
Merry, merry, merry, merry Christmas.

On, on they send
On without end
Their joyful tone
To ev'ry home

Ding, dong, ding, dong.

Who?

"Carol of the Bells" has a long history of transformation. Ukrainian music teacher Mykola Leontovich was commissioned to write a choral piece based on local folk tunes. When Peter Wilhousky, a Ukrainian-American choral director, heard the finished version, he was inspired to translate it and rewrite it into the carol we know today.

What?

The chant that became "Shchedryk" was first sung among pagan peoples. The name translates as "Generous One" or "Bountiful," and it fits in with pagan beliefs that rituals performed in midwinter would assure the return of the sun.

A later version, the one adapted by Leontovich, depicts a bluebird flying into a family's house and flitting from room to room, proclaiming that wealth and better times lie ahead. Children sang it as a New Year's song, dancing from house to house, predicting rosy futures for the householders and receiving treats in return.

This optimism for the future made it a popular nationalist song when the Ukraine briefly split from the Soviet Union.

The chant has gone through several transformations and is now a firm part of the Christmas canon. In other words, what was once pagan has now been redeemed—and isn't that what Christmas is all about?

When?

"Shchedryk," a Ukrainian song and the basis for this carol, was written in 1916 from a much older, pre-Christian era chant. It was translated and rewritten as "Carol of the Bells" in 1921.

In 1921 Georgia was invaded by Bolshevist Russia; Warren Harding became the twenty-ninth U.S. president; and Margaret Gorman won the Atlantic City Pageant Golden Mermaid trophy. The next year, she was crowned as the first Miss America.

Where?

The traditional piece that became "Shchedryk" was a very ancient chant believed to be Ukrainian in origin. Leontovich's version was first performed by his students in Kiev University. Peter Wilhousky heard the song when the Ukrainian National Chorus performed it in New York's Carnegie Hall as part of their American tour.

Why?

Perhaps inspired by a Slavic legend that all the bells in the world rang on the night Jesus was born, Wilhousky's lyrics are all about the bells spreading the Good News "o'er hill and dale" and "on without end."

Leontovich's arrangement, with separate choral groups singing against each other, probably reminded Wilhousky of the pealing or "caroling" of church bells. The word *caroling* to describe the sound of bells is, after all, the root of the word *carol*.

16   IT CAME UPON A MIDNIGHT CLEAR

It came upon a midnight clear,
That glorious song of old,
From angels bending near the earth,
To touch their harps of gold;
"Peace on the earth, good will to men,
From Heaven's all gracious King."
The world in solemn stillness lay,
To hear the angels sing.

Still through the cloven skies they come
With peaceful wings unfurled,
And still their heavenly music floats
O'er all the weary world;
Above its sad and lowly plains,
They bend on hovering wing,
And ever o'er its Babel sounds
The blessed angels sing.

Yet with the woes of sin and strife
The world has suffered long;
Beneath the angel strain have rolled
Two thousand years of wrong;
And man, at war with man, hears not
The love song which they bring;
O hush the noise, ye men of strife
And hear the angels sing.

O ye, beneath life's crushing load,
Whose forms are bending low,
Who toil along the climbing way
With painful steps and slow,
Look now, for glad and golden hours
Come swiftly on the wing.
O rest beside the weary road,
And hear the angels sing!

For lo! the days are hastening on,
By prophet-bards foretold,
When with the ever-circling years
Comes round the Age of Gold;
When peace shall over all the earth
Its ancient splendors fling,
And the whole world send back the song
Which now the angels sing.

Who?

Edmund H. Sears was a Unitarian minister. He grew up on a farm and claimed to always have a poem singing through his head while he worked. He did missionary work in the frontier lands of Ohio and afterward took a parish in his home state of Massachusetts.

Richard Storrs Willis, who wrote the music, was a Massachusetts boy who studied in Germany and became a friend of the great composer Felix Mendelssohn. Willis went on to become a music critic for the *New York Tribune*.

What?

"It Came upon a Midnight Clear" was first performed at a Sunday school Christmas performance.

Though written for children, the lyrics work for all ages. They tell of a weary world and a weary man (perhaps Sears himself). The answer to war and sin, on both a worldwide and personal level, comes when the angels rend the sky to proclaim the birth of Christ.

The carol ends with the reassurance that the "Age of Gold" is coming, as was foretold. Then the world and individuals will find a peace that will set them both to singing.

When?

"It Came upon a Midnight Clear" first appeared in print in 1849. In that year, Elizabeth Blackwell became the United States' first female doctor; Zachary Taylor, the twelfth president of the United States, refused to be sworn into office on a Sunday; and the Mississippi levee broke, flooding most of New Orleans.

Where?

After a successful ministry in Lancaster, Massachusetts, Sears had something of a breakdown. He returned to Wayland, where he had previously preached, and settled into a smaller parish with a gentler workload. The lessened pressures gave Sears more time for writing, and "It Came upon a Midnight Clear" became the most remembered product of this period.

Why?

As a student, Sears had already written a hymn that appeared in many hymnals; but "Calm on the Listening Ear of Night" is hardly ever heard now. It may, however, have provided the starting point for "It Came upon a Midnight Clear."

Sears was suffering a bout of melancholy when he wrote his most famous hymn. Europe was in a time of revolution, and the U.S. had recently been at war with Mexico. Sears's world must have seemed very far from the message of love and hope his Lord had brought.

From those dark days came a carol that still inspires people more than a century and a half later.

 ## AWAY IN A MANGER

Away in a manger,
No crib for His bed
The little Lord Jesus
Laid down His sweet head

The stars in the bright sky
Looked down where He lay
The little Lord Jesus
Asleep on the hay

The cattle are lowing
The poor Baby wakes
But little Lord Jesus
No crying He makes

I love Thee, Lord Jesus
Look down from the sky
And stay by my side,
'Til morning is nigh.

Be near me, Lord Jesus,
I ask Thee to stay
Close by me forever
And love me I pray.

Bless all the dear children
In Thy tender care
And take us to heaven
To live with Thee there.

Who?

No one knows who first composed this beautiful carol. It is believed to have been written in at least three sections at three different times, but authorship of those sections cannot be confirmed.

What?

"Away in a Manger" has as valid a claim as any to being the first carol most children learn. It is often sung to little ones before they can sing for themselves.

The first two verses of "Away in a Manger"

are the ones usually credited to Luther. In *Dainty Songs for Little Lads and Lasses,* the carol is titled "Luther's Cradle Song," without actually naming Luther as the author. Instead, initials matching the name of the book's compiler, James R. Murray, appear next to the piece. It may well be that Murray wrote the piece and dedicated it to the great reformer—but we will never know.

Perhaps a carol that so speaks to the soul and so perfectly encapsulates Jesus' call for us to come to Him as children should best be left in the mists of anonymity. Then it can be seen, as Jesus was, as a Christmas gift to all the world.

When?

In 1885, the year when "Away in a Manger was written, President Chester A. Arthur dedicated the Washington Monument; Louis Pasteur succeeded in safely vaccinating a boy against rabies; and the world's first skyscraper (with ten floors) was built in Chicago.

Where?

Though popular legend has it first being sung in Germany, "Away in a Manger" actually made its first appearance in print in the United States. In 1885 the carol appeared in a Lutheran Sunday school hymnbook, *The Little Children's Book for Schools and Families.*

Two years later it appeared in *Dainty Songs for Little Lads and Lassies,* compiled by James R. Murray. Since then, its fame has spread around the world.

Why?

Without knowing who wrote the carol, it would be difficult to know *why* it was written; but it would be safe to assume it was written as a faith-filled lullaby for little children. Indeed, the most tenacious legend surrounding the song attributes authorship to Martin Luther, who is said to have composed it for his own children.

Extensive research turned up no proof of Luther's authorship, but the idea persists, perhaps because the theme seems to fit so well with Luther's belief that all comfort is to be found in God.

WHAT CHILD IS THIS?

What Child is this who, laid to rest,
On Mary's lap is sleeping?
Whom angels greet with anthems sweet,
While shepherds watch are keeping?
This, this is Christ the King,
Whom shepherds guard and angels sing;
Haste, haste, to bring Him laud,
The Babe, the Son of Mary.

Why lies He in such mean estate,
Where ox and ass are feeding?
Good Christians, fear, for sinners here
The silent Word is pleading.
Nails, spear shall pierce Him through,
The cross be borne for me, for you.
Hail, hail the Word made flesh,
The Babe, the Son of Mary.

So bring Him incense, gold and myrrh,
Come peasant, king to own Him;
The King of kings salvation brings,
Let loving hearts enthrone Him.
Raise, raise a song on high,

The virgin sings her lullaby.
Joy, joy for Christ is born,
The Babe, the Son of Mary.

Who?

William Chatterton Dix was born in England in 1837. He seems to have inherited the habit of mixing hard, practical work from his father, John Dix, who was a surgeon and a writer.

William Dix moved from the family home in the south of England to Glasgow, Scotland, where he worked in a maritime insurance company. He was eventually promoted to manager of the company.

Dix wrote many other hymns in addition to "What Child Is This?" including, "As With Gladness Men of Old" and "Alleluia! Sing to Jesus!"

What?

"What Child Is This?" tells of the birth of the Savior. It's a beautiful scene, but Dix reminds us that Jesus has suffering in His future. There will be hardships to go through, but the end result will be glory and better times for all mankind. No doubt the words, as he wrote them in the depths of his despair, inspired Dix and reminded him that he, too, had better times ahead—both in this life and the next!

When?

"What Child Is This?" was written in 1865, the same year in which Robert E. Lee became general-in-chief of the Confederate forces in the American Civil War. Later that year, he surrendered to Union general Ulysses S. Grant. Also in 1865, President Abraham Lincoln was assassinated; and The Christian Mission, which later became The Salvation Army, was founded in London.

Where?

Born in Bristol, England, Dix spent most of his working life in Glasgow, Scotland. At the time, Glasgow was a major shipping and shipbuilding port. Maritime insurance was a sound way for a hard-working young man to make a living for himself.

"What Child Is This?" was first published in 1871, in *Christmas Carols, New and Old*.

Why?

A man of strong faith and considerable poetic talent, Dix nevertheless was busy with employment in an industry not generally conducive to creativity.

When he was twenty-nine, he was stricken with a serious illness, which left him bedridden for many months. The extra free time might have been conducive to creativity, but the combination of the illness, being so far from home, and worries about his job led him to fall into a depression.

Dix recovered, but the unexpected harvest that grew from the seeds of his depression were several hymns of praise and devotion, some of which are still sung today.

 ## THE BIRTHDAY OF A KING

In the little village of Bethlehem,
There lay a Child one day;
And the sky was bright with a holy light
O'er the place where Jesus lay.

Alleluia! O how the angels sang.
Alleluia! How it rang!
And the sky was bright with a holy light
'Twas the birthday of a King.

'Twas a humble birthplace, but O how much
God gave to us that day,
From the manger bed what a path has led,
What a perfect, holy way.

Alleluia! O how the angels sang.
Alleluia! How it rang!
And the sky was bright with a holy light
'Twas the birthday of a King.

Who?

William Harold Neidlinger was a composer and music teacher. He played the organ at St. Michael's Church in New York City and conducted several choirs. His book *Small Songs for Small Singers* may have been the catalyst for an interest in child psychology. He eventually gave up music altogether and established a school for disabled children in New Jersey.

What?

Neidlinger's carol is a reminder, for children and adults, that although we celebrate the birth of a child in the Nativity, and although that is a gentle, wonderful moment in history, we should never forget that the child was also a king. Not just a king—but the King of kings!

When?

"The Birthday of a King" is believed to have been written around 1890. In that year, Idaho and Wyoming became states, and the comic actor Stan Laurel (Arthur Stanley Jefferson) was born in England.

Where?

"The Birthday of a King" was most likely written in Philadelphia, where Neidlinger conducted the Mannheim Glee Club.

Why?

"The Birthday of a King" is a simple but beautiful song and may be a precursor of Neidlinger's passion for writing songs for children. In 1896 he published a collection called *Small Songs for Small Singers,* which became a standard in kindergartens across the country.

12 ONCE IN ROYAL DAVID'S CITY

Once in royal David's city
Stood a lowly cattle shed,
Where a mother laid her Baby
In a manger for His bed:
Mary was that mother mild,
Jesus Christ her little Child.

He came down to earth from Heaven,
Who is God and Lord of all,
And His shelter was a stable,
And His cradle was a stall;
With the poor, and mean, and lowly,
Lived on earth our Savior holy.

And, through all His wondrous childhood,
He would honor and obey,
Love and watch the lowly maiden,
In whose gentle arms He lay:
Christian children all must be
Mild, obedient, good as He.

For He is our childhood's pattern;
Day by day, like us He grew;

He was little, weak and helpless,
Tears and smiles like us He knew;
And He feeleth for our sadness,
And He shareth in our gladness.

And our eyes at last shall see Him,
Through His own redeeming love,
For that Child so dear and gentle
Is our Lord in Heav'n above,
And He leads His children on
To the place where He is gone.

Not in that poor lowly stable,
With the oxen standing by,
We shall see Him; but in Heaven,
Set at God's right hand on high;
Where like stars His children crowned
All in white shall wait around.

Who?

Cecil Frances Humphries was the daughter of a British army major stationed in Dublin, Ireland. She married the Reverend William Alexander, who went on to become bishop of Derry in Northern Ireland.

Humphries wrote many other hymns, including "All Things Bright and Beautiful" and "There Is a Green Hill Far Away."

What?

The city mentioned in song isn't Jerusalem, where David was king. It's Bethlehem, where both David and Jesus were born. The carol is a reminder of the miracle that took place in Bethlehem and a reminder to children everywhere that in Jesus they have a role model worth following.

The fact that "Once in Royal David's City" is thought of as a children's carol has not deterred adults from enjoying it. Humphries may encourage children to be "mild, obedient, good as He," so they will in good time join David and his Lord gathered around God's throne. But it's a lesson not wasted on listeners of any age. After all, we are called to come to Jesus as children; and, in the presence of the Father, well, how else should we be?

When?

"Once in Royal David's City" was first published in 1848. That same year, the California Gold Rush began; several women publicly wore bloomers at a feminist rally; and the first medical school for women was established in Boston.

Also in 1848, Ireland, where the composer of this hymn lived, was in the midst of a potato famine; Karl Marx and Friedrich Engels published

The Communist Manifesto; and Belle Starr, the notorious outlaw, was born.

Where?

The book *Hymns for Little Children,* which contains "Once in Royal David's City," was printed in Dublin when Humphries lived there just before her marriage.

Why?

Aside from the obvious personal faith demonstrated in the carol, Humphries's motivation may be discerned from the dedication she placed inside *Hymns for Little Children.* She dedicated the book to her godchildren, "hoping that the language of verse which children love may help to impress on their minds what they are, what I have promised for them, and what they must seek to be." In other words, Humphries was writing to remind her young readers that they were children of God.

The proceeds of this and other books by Humphries helped children who would never hear her songs. The income from her writing went toward setting up and supporting a school for deaf children.

11   O COME, ALL YE FAITHFUL

O come, all ye faithful, joyful and triumphant,
O come ye, O come ye, to Bethlehem.
Come and behold Him, born the King of angels;

Chorus
O come, let us adore Him,
O come, let us adore Him,
O come, let us adore Him,
Christ the Lord.

God of God, Light of Light,
Lo! He abhors not the Virgin's womb;
Very God, begotten not created.

Chorus

Sing, choirs of angels, sing in exultation;
Sing, all ye citizens of heaven above!
Glory to God, in the highest.

Chorus

Yea, Lord, we greet Thee, born this happy morning;
Jesus, to Thee be glory given;
Word of the Father, now in flesh appearing.

Who?

A supporter of Bonnie Prince Charlie, John Francis Wade fled England after the 1745 Jacobite Rebellion failed disastrously. He settled in Douay, France, with other exiled Catholics and spent the rest of his days there working as a music teacher.

What?

"O Come, All Ye Faithful" is an early example of a first-class conspiracy theory. Wade's published collections of hymns were always beautifully decorated and supposedly made lavish use of Jacobite imagery. The song's lyrics were thought by some to be a coded message to fellow sympathizers who wanted to see a Catholic monarch back on the throne of Great Britain.

According to the theory, "Bethlehem" was a well-known code word for England, and "angelorum"—*angels* in the hymn—would be replaced with "Anglorum," meaning "English." Thus, "born the King of angels" became "born the king of the English" and referred to Bonnie Prince Charlie.

It's possible the song had a hidden meaning back in the mid-eighteenth century. Today, however, it is the obvious, face-value meaning that makes the carol so very loved and so often sung around the world.

Wade may have been part of a conspiracy, but it's more likely he was simply a man of God celebrating the birth of his Savior and wanting to share that feeling with the *all* the faithful.

When?

"O Come, All Ye Faithful" was first printed in 1751, the same year that Benjamin Franklin was given permission by the Philadelphia legislature to set up the first hospital in the colonies. Also, James Madison, the fourth president of the United States, was born in 1751; and Georgetown was founded on the shores of the Potomac.

Where?

"Adeste Fidelis," the Latin original of "O Come, All Ye Faithful," was published by John Francis Wade in 1751, in his collection *Cantus Diversi.* Wade was living in France at the time and was never able to return to England.

Why?

A hymn writer before his ill-advised political allegiance forced him to flee his home country,

Wade continued to write while abroad. Communication was not a problem, because French was the language of the English educated classes at the time, and Latin was the common language of faith and hymn writing across Europe. Wade supplemented his teaching income by hand copying or translating Latin hymns and selling them to private buyers for their personal worship.

10 GOD REST YOU MERRY, GENTLEMEN

God rest you merry, gentlemen,
Let nothing you dismay,
Remember Christ our Savior
Was born on Christmas day,
To save us all from Satan's pow'r
When we were gone astray.

Chorus
O tidings of comfort and joy,
Comfort and joy,
O tidings of comfort and joy.

From God our heavenly Father
A blessed angel came.
And unto certain shepherds

Brought tidings of the same,
How that in Bethlehem was born
The Son of God by name:

Chorus

The shepherds at those tidings
Rejoiced much in mind,
And left their flocks a-feeding,
In tempest, storm, and wind,
And went to Bethlehem straightway
This blessed babe to find:

Chorus

But when to Bethlehem they came,
Whereat this infant lay
They found him in a manger,
Where oxen feed on hay;
His mother Mary kneeling,
Unto the Lord did pray:

Chorus

Now to the Lord sing praises,
All you within this place,
And with true love and brotherhood
Each other now embrace;
This holy tide of Christmas
All others doth deface:

Chorus

Who?

No one knows who first came up with "God Rest
You Merry, Gentlemen," but educated guesses can
be made as to the separate origins of the melody
and the words.

What?

We might think the "gentlemen" were merry, but
it was their *rest* that actually should have been
merry. The placing of the comma gives it away.

The watchmen, in the nights leading up
to Christmas, were singing to their patrons of
the birth of their Redeemer, and in His name
were encouraging people to love each other. Jesus, they sang, had saved them all from Satan's
power. With that in mind, they had every reason
to rest merrily and safely in their beds.

In taking the news of Christ's birth into the
frosty streets, those unknown watchmen may
well have been the world's first Christmas carolers. If they could have foreseen how popular that
tradition would become, they would probably
have been very merry gentlemen indeed!

When?

In 1833, the year in which "God Rest You Merry,
Gentlemen" was written, the English Parliament

passed the Slavery Abolition Act; 350 settlers established what would become the city of Chicago; Alfred Nobel, the creator of dynamite and founder of the Nobel Peace Prize, was born; and Andrew Jackson began his second term as president of the United States.

Where?

The melody for "God Rest You Merry, Gentlemen" may have originally been paired with other lyrics. It was known in France and may have been taken to the English West Country by French merchants. There it met a long-established English lyric.

The lyrics and melody were published together for the first time in *Christmas Carols Ancient and Modern*.

Why?

In days gone by, towns often had walls with gates that were closed at night. There was also an ever-present risk of fire. A spilled lamp might set a thatched-roofed home ablaze, and that home might be pressed up against another just like it. So, the town's merchants and nobility would hire watchmen to patrol the streets while the rest of the town slept. At the first sign of anything amiss, they would

The heavenly Babe you there shall find
To human view displayed,
All meanly wrapped in swaddling bands,
And in a manger laid.
Thus spake the Seraph, and forthwith
Appeared a heavenly throng
Of Angels praising God and thus,
Addressed their joyful song.

All glory be to God on high,
And to the earth be peace;
Goodwill henceforth from heaven to men
Begin and never cease, begin and never cease!

Who?

Nahum Tate was the son of an Irish vicar. He moved to London to try to make a living as a poet. He found success as a playwright, even adapting Shakespeare's plays in an early attempt at political correctness. His determination to make sure as many scenes as possible dignified the crown and the government was recognized when he was appointed poet laureate, or the monarch's poet.

In his time, Tate revolutionized hymn singing in the Church of England.

What?

"While Shepherds Watched Their Flocks" was the first nonpsalm song recognized as worthy of singing in church by the Church of England.

Aware of the sensibilities involved and not wanting to upset worshippers too much, Tate didn't stray far from Scripture. "While Shepherds Watched Their Flocks" is simply a retelling of the Nativity as it was recorded in Luke 2:8–14. Tate simply took the amazement of the shepherds and the rejoicing of the angels and fit it into a beautiful melody.

The carol ends with the angelic proclamation of goodwill to all men. Unfortunately, the goodwill of Tate's fellow men would soon run out. He died a debtor, seeking sanctuary in the Royal Mint.

No doubt he would have been delighted to find that goodwill renewed in heaven, where he would find that all his debts were already paid!

When?

"While Shepherds Watched Their Flocks" was first published in 1702, the same year that the earliest known English language newspaper, *The Daily Courant*, was published in London.

Also in 1702, William of Orange died from

injuries suffered in a fall from his horse, and the British crown was transferred to his sister-in-law, Anne.

Queen Anne's War, the second of five wars between the British, French, and Spanish for control of North America, also began that year.

Where?

Working with Nicholas Brady, who had been chaplain to King William and now filled the same role for Queen Anne, Tate published the *New Version of the Psalms of David* in London. "While Shepherds Watched Their Flocks" appeared in a supplement to this book.

Why?

Prior to 1700, the only songs allowed to be sung in the Church of England were either the Psalms or other compositions of Scripture. Brady and Tate's *New Version of the Psalms of David* worked toward the relaxation of this rule by adapting the Psalms to make them easier to sing.

THE FIRST NOEL

The first Noel, the angels did say
Was to certain poor shepherds in fields as they lay
In fields where they lay keeping their sheep
On a cold winter's night that was so deep.
Noel, Noel, Noel, Noel
Born is the King of Israel!

They looked up and saw a star
Shining in the East beyond them far
And to the earth it gave great light
And so it continued both day and night.
Noel, Noel, Noel, Noel
Born is the King of Israel!

And by the light of that same star
Three wise men came from country far
To seek for a king was their intent
And to follow the star wherever it went.
Noel, Noel, Noel, Noel
Born is the King of Israel!

This star drew nigh to the northwest
O'er Bethlehem it took its rest

And there it did both pause and stay
Right o'er the place where Jesus lay.
Noel, Noel, Noel, Noel
Born is the King of Israel!

Then entered in those wise men three
Full reverently upon their knee
And offered there in His presence
Their gold and myrrh and frankincense.
Noel, Noel, Noel, Noel
Born is the King of Israel!

Then let us all with one accord
Sing praises to our heavenly Lord
That hath made heaven and earth of nought
And with his blood mankind has bought.
Noel, Noel, Noel, Noel
Born is the King of Israel!

Who?

Given the traditional rivalry between England and France, it is perhaps unsurprising that both countries claim this carol as one of their traditional songs.

What?

While the preponderance of opinion suggests "The First Noel" is an English carol, the word *noel* is definitely French. But even there, opinions vary as to its meaning. Some say it comes from *natalis,* meaning "birth," but the ancient Gallic (French) expression *neu helle* might be a more likely candidate.

The pagan Gauls celebrated Neu-helle as part of their midwinter festival. It means "new light," which is what they must have been hoping for during the short, dark days of winter.

Since then, of course, a new Light had come into the world. So whether the carol is French or English, whether *noel* means "birth" or "new light," it doesn't really matter. What matters is the One of whom the song speaks, the One whom angels, shepherds, and magi came to see: Jesus Christ, born to be the light of the world.

When?

"The First Noel" is traditional but was first published in 1823. That year, eleven-year-old Franz Liszt gave a piano recital. Afterward, he was congratulated by no less than Ludwig van Beethoven. Also in 1823, Joseph Smith said that God directed him to where the Book of Mormon was found inscribed on tablets of gold.

Where?

When trying to determine the original home of "The First Noel," much is made of the spelling of the word *noel*. Had it been British, the word would have been spelled "nowell." Unfortunately, centuries of conquest and intermarriage meant that the language of the ruling and educated classes on both sides of the English Channel was French! However, the version sung today is generally accepted as being Cornish in origin.

"The First Noel" was preserved and printed in *Some Ancient Christmas Carols with the Tunes to Which They Were Formerly Sung in the West of England* by Davies Gilbert.

Why?

"The First Noel" was part of a European tradition of mystery plays. The central mystery to these public performances was the miracle of how God became man and why He would make such a sacrifice for us.

Essentially, they were a retelling of the Nativity in a way that everyone could hear and understand. Occasionally they became the subject of intertown rivalries, with each town insisting its play was the best; but more often they were a public display of thanks and devotion.

7   O HOLY NIGHT

O holy night! The stars are brightly shining,
It is the night of the dear Saviour's birth.
Long lay the world in sin and error pining.
Till He appeared and the soul felt its worth.
A thrill of hope the weary world rejoices,
For yonder breaks a new and glorious morn.
Fall on your knees! Oh, hear the angel voices!
O night divine, the night when Christ was born;
O night, O Holy Night, O night divine!
O night, O Holy Night, O night divine!

Led by the light of faith serenely beaming,
With glowing hearts by His cradle we stand.
O'er the world a star is sweetly gleaming,
Now come the wise men from out of the Orient land.
The King of kings lay thus in lowly manger;
In all our trials born to be our Friend!
He knows our need, our weakness is no stranger.
Behold your King! Before Him lowly bend!
Behold your King! Before Him lowly bend!

Truly He taught us to love one another,
His law is love and His gospel is peace.

Chains He shall break, for the slave is our brother.
And in His name all oppression shall cease.
Sweet hymns of joy in grateful chorus raise we,
With all our hearts we praise His holy name.
Christ is the Lord! Then ever, ever praise we,
His power and glory ever more proclaim!
His power and glory ever more proclaim!

Who?

Placide Cappeau de Roquemaure was a sporadic churchgoer who later gave up attending altogether. He was the son of a cooper and probably would have followed in his father's trade of making wine barrels had a friend not accidentally shot him in the hand when he was eight.

Freed from any expectation of manual work, and aided by compensation from his friend's family, Cappeau received a good education. He became a novelist, a poet, and an artist, despite having only one hand.

What?

"O Holy Night" is a beautifully poetic expression of faith, despite the uncertainty of its author's religious stance.

After the French church banned the carol, it was given a new lease on life in America where the line "Chains he shall break, for the slave is our brother" made it somewhat of an anthem among abolitionists.

In a precursor to the more famous World War I Christmas truce, a young French soldier stepped into "no man's land" in 1871 and serenaded his Prussian enemies with "O Holy Night."

On Christmas Eve 1906, Reginald Fessenden made what may well have been the first radio broadcast of speech and music. He quoted from the Gospel of Luke (on which Cappeau based his poem), then took out his violin and played "O Holy Night."

Cappeau may well have been an unlikely candidate to bring such a beautiful, faith-filled carol to the world; but a quick look at the Bible will tell you that unlikely candidates are the ones God likes the best!

When?

"O Holy Night" was written in 1847. That same year, Samuel Colt sold his revolving barrel pistol to the U.S. government; the California town of Yerba Buena was renamed San Francisco; the United States issued its first postage stamps; and Brigham Young established Salt Lake City.

Where?

Cappeau claimed he wrote "Minuit Chretiens," or "O Holy Night," during a stagecoach journey to Paris. Perhaps the lack of a traveling companion allowed divine inspiration to do its work.

Why?

Knowing Cappeau's literary abilities, the local priest asked him to write a carol for Christmas. Cappeau himself seems to have been impressed by the outcome and he rushed to have his composer friend Adolphe-Charles Adam put a suitable tune to the piece.

The carol was immediately popular, but when it came out that Cappeau was (by then) a socialist nonchurchgoer and Adam was Jewish, the French church banned it for a time.

6 JOY TO THE WORLD

Joy to the world, the Lord is come!
Let earth receive her King;
Let every heart prepare Him room,
And Heaven and nature sing,
And Heaven and nature sing,
And Heaven, and Heaven, and nature sing.

Joy to the earth, the Savior reigns!
Let men their songs employ;
While fields and floods, rocks, hills and plains
Repeat the sounding joy,
Repeat the sounding joy,
Repeat, repeat, the sounding joy.

No more let sins and sorrows grow,
Nor thorns infest the ground;
He comes to make His blessings flow
Far as the curse is found,
Far as the curse is found,
Far as, far as, the curse is found.

He rules the world with truth and grace,
And makes the nations prove

The glories of His righteousness,
And wonders of His love,
And wonders of His love,
And wonders, wonders, of His love.

Who?

Isaac Watts is known as the father of English hymnody. He was the first prolific hymn writer to emerge after Nahum Tate had created an environment in which such a thing could happen. Watts wrote more than 750 hymns, many of which are still popular today.

An inveterate rhymer as a child, Watts was punished for speaking in verse. When he then appealed his punishment in verse, he earned another punishment!

Watts left behind a massive body of work, which is currently in the care of Yale University.

What?

Watts gives a nod toward the older tradition of singing only the Psalms by vaguely acknowledging Psalm 98, but he was more concerned with singing songs of "Christian experience."

The experience he writes about in "Joy to the World" is one that Christians everywhere eagerly anticipate.

Despite being adopted as a popular Christmas song, the coming of Christ to which Watts refers is not His birth. There is nothing of the Nativity in "Joy to the World," no shepherds, no manger, no wise men. Watts has "heaven and nature" singing for the Second Coming of the Lord, when mankind will be free from the curse placed on Adam.

The world should be a joyful place at Christmas, but it isn't always so. When Jesus comes back, though, as Isaac Watts points out, the joy of the whole world will be unrestrained. Even the rocks will sing!

When?

In 1719, the year "Joy to the World" was written, Daniel Defoe published *Robinson Crusoe,* based on the self-imposed abandonment of Scottish sailor Alexander Selkirk on an uninhabited island.

The *American Weekly Mercury,* Pennsylvania's first newspaper, was published in 1719; and the father of Wolfgang Amadeus Mozart was born.

Where?

Watts was born in Southampton, England, in the house of a father who was twice jailed for his nonconformist views. Watts followed his father's nonconformist path, but avoided the jail sentences.

"Joy to the World" was published in Watts's collection *The Psalms of David: Imitated in the Language of the New Testament, and Applied to the Christian State and Worship.* At the time, he was living in Stoke-Newington, England.

Why?

Isaac Watts was a young man when Nahum Tate's work allowed for the singing of hymns other than the Psalms in the Church of England. A prolific poet and man of (nonconformist) faith, Watts was the right man at the right time to get the English hymn writing tradition off to a good start.

5 AS WITH GLADNESS MEN OF OLD

As with gladness, men of old
Did the guiding star behold
As with joy they hailed its light
Leading onward, beaming bright
So, most glorious Lord, may we
Evermore be led to Thee.

As with joyful steps they sped
To that lowly manger bed
There to bend the knee before
Him Whom Heaven and earth adore;
So may we with willing feet
Ever seek Thy mercy seat.

As they offered gifts most rare
At that manger rude and bare;
So may we with holy joy,
Pure and free from sin's alloy,
All our costliest treasures bring,
Christ, to Thee, our heavenly King.

Holy Jesus, every day
Keep us in the narrow way;

And, when earthly things are past,
Bring our ransomed souls at last
Where they need no star to guide,
Where no clouds Thy glory hide.

In the heavenly country bright,
Need they no created light;
Thou its Light, its Joy, its Crown,
Thou its Sun which goes not down;
There forever may we sing
Alleluias to our King!

Who?

Born to a well-to-do family, William Chatterton Dix might have had more leisure to write than the average person. As it was, he had to make a living for himself and thus managed a marine insurance company in Glasgow. Despite his time-consuming occupation, he still managed to produce and publish four collections of hymns, publishing the first when he was twenty-four.

Dix also wrote "To Thee, O Lord, Our Hearts We Raise" and "Come Unto Me, Ye Weary."

What?

In "As with Gladness, Men of Old," Dix refers to the joy and excitement of the magi as they follow the star to Bethlehem. Then he describes how those wise men gave of their very best. Given that Jesus still lives and saves today, Dix asks, why should anyone be less glad than those who first encountered Him? If He is no less alive and His work is no less powerful, why then should our excitement be any less?

The carol ends with a plea to "keep us in the narrow way" until we reach the place where we can sing our alleluias to Jesus in person. Dix's way must have felt very straitened in his sickbed, but the joy of the magi, the light of the star, and his love of the Lord helped him pull through.

Dix lived to glorify God for many more years. And he surely did that with gladness, just like the men of old!

When?

"As with Gladness, Men of Old" was written in 1860, the same year that Abraham Lincoln was elected president of the United States without the votes of a single Southern state. The South began seceding from the union shortly afterward.

Also in 1860 the Oxford University Museum played host to the first major debate on the theory of evolution.

Where?

"As with Gladness, Men of Old" first appeared in print in the collection *Hymns of Love and Joy,* but it was written while Dix lay in bed in Glasgow making a long recovery from a life-threatening illness.

Why?

Suffering from depression after his long illness, Dix wrote about a world without hope—until Jesus came! Even in his own darkest moment, Dix knew he was saved and that Jesus was the reason why. If he would not have recovered, there was still heaven to look forward to.

Realizing it was Epiphany, the day tradition-ally celebrated as the one on which the magi found the Christ child, Dix turned his attention to what a wonderful experience that must have been.

4 LO, HOW A ROSE E'ER BLOOMING

*Lo, how a Rose e'er blooming from tender stem hath
      sprung!
Of Jesse's lineage coming, as men of old have sung.
It came, a floweret bright, amid the cold of winter,
When half spent was the night.*

*Isaiah 'twas foretold it, the Rose I have in mind;
With Mary we behold it, the virgin mother kind.
To show God's love aright, she bore to men a Savior,
When half spent was the night.*

*The shepherds heard the story proclaimed by angels
      bright,
How Christ, the Lord of glory, was born on earth
      this night.
To Bethlehem they sped and in the manger found
      Him,
As angel heralds said.*

*This Flower, whose fragrance tender with
      sweetness fills the air,
Dispels with glorious splendor the darkness
      everywhere;*

raise the alarm, otherwise they might announce the time on the hour with a call of "All's well!"

At some point, the watchmen, perhaps bored by the monotony, or perhaps fueled by a drink or two, started singing. If they sang well, doubtless there would be an extra coin or two in their purse at the end of the week.

9 WHILE SHEPHERDS WATCHED THEIR FLOCKS

While shepherds watched their flocks by night,
All seated on the ground,
The angel of the Lord came down,
And glory shone around.

Fear not, said he, for mighty dread
Had seized their troubled mind.
Glad tidings of great joy I bring
To you and all mankind.

To you, in David's town, this day
Is born of David's line
A Saviour, which is Christ the Lord,
And this shall be the sign.

True Man, yet very God, from sin and death He
saves us,
And lightens every load.

O Savior, Child of Mary, who felt our human woe,
O Savior, King of glory, who dost our weakness know;
Bring us at length we pray, to the bright courts of
Heaven,
And to the endless day!

Who?

According to tradition, the carol was created by a German monk, who, while walking in the snow, found a rose in full bloom.

The song was translated into English in 1894 by Theodore Baker, an American music editor who studied and lived in Germany.

The melody, thought to be at least as old as the lyric, was adapted and put together with the words by Michael Praetorius, who composed music for many Lutheran hymns.

What?

During the German Reformation, many of those who would become Protestants had been brought up on Catholic tradition and still had a fondness for many of the hymns. "Lo, How a Rose

E'er Blooming" is one of the hymns that made the transition.

The emphasis was changed from the Song of Solomon's rose of Sharon to Isaiah's branch from the stump of Jesse. In other words, from the mother of Jesus to Jesus Himself.

This transition was made all the easier because, in the earliest known manuscript, the written word might have been either *reis* (branch) or *ros* (rose).

"Lo, How a Rose E'er Blooming" came from an uncertain beginning. It has been translated and adapted many times and pulled this way and that by different churches. It should be a mess. Instead, like that rosebud daring to open in the snow or that baby hunted by a king soon after He was born, it defied the odds to become something very special indeed.

When?

"Lo, How a Rose E'er Blooming" is believed to be a fifteenth-century German carol. During this period, the papacy was split in two; Columbus sailed for the West Indies; and the Incas ruled South America. This era is generally considered to be a transition period between the Middle Ages and the early Renaissance.

"Es Ist Ein Reis Entsprungen," the German original of "Lo, How a Rose E'er Blooming," was included in the collection *Gebetbuchlein des Frater Conradus,* published in 1582.

In 1599 a twenty-three-stanza version of the carol was published in *Alte Catholische Geistliche Kirchengeseng,* in Cologne.

Where?
Traditionally, Trier, Germany, near the Luxembourg border.

Why?
The monk who found the rose is supposed to have plucked it and taken it back to his monastery. There he placed it before the altar and dedicated it to Mary, the mother of Jesus (sometimes referred to as the Rose of Sharon). The carol is a simple, but lengthy, song of devotion referring to the Song of Solomon.

3) LO, HE COMES WITH CLOUDS DESCENDING

Lo! He comes with clouds descending,
Once for favored sinners slain;
Thousand thousand saints attending,
Swell the triumph of His train:
Hallelujah! Hallelujah! Hallelujah!
God appears on earth to reign.

Every eye shall now behold Him
Robed in dreadful majesty;
Those who set at naught and sold Him,
Pierced and nailed Him to the tree,
Deeply wailing, deeply wailing, deeply wailing,
Shall the true Messiah see.

Every island, sea, and mountain,
Heav'n and earth, shall flee away;
All who hate Him must, confounded,
Hear the trump proclaim the day:
Come to judgment! Come to judgment! Come to judgment!
Come to judgment! Come away!

Now redemption, long expected,
See in solemn pomp appear;

All His saints, by man rejected,
Now shall meet Him in the air:
Hallelujah! Hallelujah! Hallelujah!
See the day of God appear!

Answer Thine own bride and Spirit,
Hasten, Lord, the general doom!
The new Heav'n and earth t'inherit,
Take Thy pining exiles home:
All creation, all creation, all creation,
Travails! groans! and bids Thee come!

The dear tokens of His passion
Still His dazzling body bears;
Cause of endless exultation
To His ransomed worshippers;
With what rapture, with what rapture, with what
        rapture
Gaze we on those glorious scars!

Yea, Amen! let all adore Thee,
High on Thine eternal throne;
Savior, take the power and glory,
Claim the kingdom for Thine own;
O come quickly! O come quickly! O come quickly!
Everlasting God, come down!

Who?

John Cennick managed to pack a lot into his thirty-seven years on earth. After a youth spent living on the seamier side of London, where he was no stranger to drinking, gambling, and stealing, he had the good fortune to bump into John Wesley.

The founder of Methodism turned Cennick's life around. Abandoning notions of being a surveyor, Cennick became the first Methodist lay preacher (though he would later follow the Moravian tradition).

Through John Wesley, Cennick met the great hymnist Charles Wesley. Charles Wesley rewrote Cennick's hymn "Lo, He Comes with Countless Trumpets," turning it into "Lo, He Comes with Clouds Descending."

The hymn was changed again by Martin Madan, another young man on whom the Wesleys had a profound influence.

What?

"Lo, He Comes with Clouds Descending" is emphatically not a Christmas song. There is no baby asleep in a manger, and no amazed shepherds or adoring parents. Jesus in this hymn is clothed in majesty, a king coming to claim His realm, expecting to be met by the faithful.

Christmas may not be the proper time to sing this song, but perhaps Cennick, Charles Wesley, and Madan would have appreciated our using the event as a rehearsal for when He really does come down through those clouds.

When?

"Lo, He Comes with Clouds Descending" was written and published in 1752. In that year, Benjamin Franklin conducted his famous electrical experiment, flying a kite with a key hanging from it in a thunderstorm.

Also in 1752, Thomas Chatterton, the English poet after whom hymnist William Chatterton Dix was named, was born; and Great Britain adopted the Gregorian calendar.

Where?

Written in London, "Lo, He Comes with Clouds Descending" was first published in Cennick's *Collection of Sacred Hymns*.

Charles Wesley published his version of the song in 1858, in *Hymns of Intercession for All Mankind*.

In Martin Madan's book *The Lock Hospital Collection*, published in 1760, we have the first instance of the hymn as we know it today.

Why?

As a recently saved sinner, Cennick must have been keen to see the Second Coming of the Lord. His original version is full of the glory that day would bring and how the wicked would wail in fear. One of the subsequent adapters softened it somewhat with an early insertion reminding the world (and perhaps Cennick) that the Lord had died for sinners. While those who had rejected Jesus had every reason to fear, those who repented would wish to hasten the day He arrived.

 I HEARD THE BELLS ON CHRISTMAS DAY

I heard the bells on Christmas day
Their old familiar carols play,
And wild and sweet the words repeat
Of peace on earth, good will to men.

And thought how, as the day had come,
The belfries of all Christendom
Had rolled along the unbroken song
Of peace on earth, good will to men.

Till ringing, singing on its way
The world revolved from night to day,
A voice, a chime, a chant sublime
Of peace on earth, good will to men.

And in despair I bowed my head
"There is no peace on earth," I said,
"For hate is strong and mocks the song
Of peace on earth, good will to men."

Then pealed the bells more loud and deep:
"God is not dead, nor doth He sleep;
The wrong shall fail, the right prevail
With peace on earth, good will to men."

Who?

Henry Wadsworth Longfellow was one of the best known American poets of the nineteenth century. He also wrote "Paul Revere's Ride" and "The Song of Hiawatha."

John Baptiste Calkin, who put Longfellow's words to music, was an English organist and professor of music.

What?

Perhaps understandably, Longfellow's "Christmas Bells" addressed the subject of mankind's dire state. "And in despair," he wrote, "I bowed my head. 'There is no peace on earth,' I said, 'for hate is strong and mocks the song of peace on earth, good will to men.'"

Despite what the poet and his country were going through at the time, the poem is one of hope and deliverance. "God is not dead," writes Longfellow, "nor doth He sleep; the wrong shall fail, the right prevail."

Twelve years later, John Baptiste Calkin rearranged "Christmas Bells." He left out the more overt references to war, making the message more universal, and set it to the tune *Waltham*. So a poem born at the height of a bloody conflict made the transition to Christmas carol.

Hope, not futility, is the message of Longfellow's poem. In singing it at Christmas, we affirm that mankind's lower nature will not win. The message of the Christmas bells is that while God loves us there is always better to come!

When?

"I Heard the Bells on Christmas Day" was written in 1864, a year before the end of the American Civil War. That same year, an Act of Congress stated that henceforth "In God We Trust" would be embossed on all U.S. coins; and the International Red Cross was founded.

Where?

Longfellow spent the latter part of life in Cambridge, Massachusetts, in a house that had once served as a headquarters for George Washington. This is where he wrote "I Heard the Bells on Christmas Day," which he originally titled "Christmas Bells."

Why?

Longfellow had achieved success, but his life had often been touched by tragedy. His first wife had suffered a miscarriage and died. Three years before he wrote "I Heard the Bells on Christmas Day," his second wife had been badly burned and died of her injuries. Then, still coping with his grief and with his country in the midst of the Civil War, he heard that his son had been wounded in battle.

Longfellow had barely written since the death of his second wife. "I Heard the Bells on Christmas Day" is a rare gift from that period in his life.

1 FOR UNTO US A CHILD IS BORN

For unto us a child is born,
To us a son is given;
The government shall rest on Him,
The anointed one from heaven.
His name is Wonderful Counsellor,
The Mighty God is He,
The Everlasting Father,
The humble Prince of Peace.

Who?

George Frideric Handel was a German-born composer who trained in Italy. In 1710 he became chapel master to the elector of Hanover, who then became King George I of Great Britain. Handel moved to London to write for the king and became a British subject. He also composed the *Water Music Suites* and *Music for the Royal Fireworks*.

Charles Jennens, a literary scholar and editor of Shakespeare's plays, wrote the libretto to Handel's *Messiah*.

What?

Though Handel's *Messiah* is widely regarded as the finest piece of music ever composed, Charles Jennens drew the words for "For Unto Us a Child Is Born" straight from the greatest book ever written—the Bible.

Handel kept revising his work and a version more familiar to the modern audience was performed as a benefit for a foundling hospital in 1750.

The performance was such a success that it was repeated every year of Handel's life. The money raised enabled the press to say, "*Messiah* has fed the hungry, clothed the naked, and fostered the orphan."

Bach and Mozart greatly admired Handel's work, and Beethoven declared him "the master of us all." But from the tears said to have flowed freely while Handel wrote his greatest work, it is likely he knew only too well that the One of whom he wrote, Jesus the Messiah, was the real master of us all.

When?

"For Unto Us a Child Is Born" was written in 1741, the same year in which the first known Europeans set foot on Alaskan soil; Benedict

Arnold, the American Revolutionary War general, was born; and Anders Celsius invented the centigrade temperature scale.

Where?

Handel composed *Messiah* at Jennens's country house in Gopsall, Leicestershire. Because the idea of staging a religious work in a public forum was considered at that time to be vaguely scandalous, *Messiah* (from which "For Unto Us a Child Is Born" is taken) was first performed in Dublin, where the London critics were unlikely to see it.

Why?

Messiah came to Handel at a low point in his career. Later, perhaps with an eye to publicity, or perhaps with utmost sincerity, he recalled writing it: "I saw the heavens opened. . .and God sitting on the throne. . . . Whether I was in my body or out of my body when I wrote it, I know not. God knows."

Messiah may have been a brilliant, if risky, career move, or it may indeed have been divinely inspired.

Keep Christ in Christmas
and in every day
of the year ahead!

One Year with Jesus
365 Thoughts on the Red Letter Words